BOOMERS
The Ageless Generation

Sell them if you can!

Meet this marketing challenge now...

BY PHIL GOODMAN
with Irene Schaffer
Edited by Lil Wagner

Published by BBP Publishers
a division of Blue Book Publishers, Inc.
7807 Girard Avenue, Suite 200
La Jolla, California 92037
ISBN 1–880846–00–4 $12.95
Printed in the United States
December, 1991
First Edition

I dedicate this book to my parents,
Archie and Sadie Goodman, whose love and devotion
gave me the confidence to succeed in life.

Increase your profits with practical strategies based on the valuable wisdom and experience of the author, who has found that:

- Boomers and their mind-set will change marketing forever.

- The radical '60s is responsible for changing your marketing in the '90s.

- Boomers and their children will spend more money in retail sales in the next three decades than all of the senior citizens in the past 100 years.

- Pay attention to the female boomer in the '90s or you'll lose the competitive edge.

- Use marketing, not psychology, to capture the boomer market in the '90s.

- Reach the boomer one day at a time, instead of banking on success predictions.

- You'll never capture the boomers if you count on the seniors as your market.

- You stand a chance of going down the tubes if you don't use radio, the boomers' medium.

- Industries that have neglected the boomer are now paying the price.

- Impulse buying, not discretionary income, will guarantee sales.

TABLE OF CONTENTS

ABOUT THE AUTHOR

Phil Goodman, President of Western Media Corporation, has been called "the guru of boomer marketing" by the National Association of Broadcasters. With 35 years of marketing experience, his focus on the boomer has been well-established. His broad-based background includes high visibility in the media's top 100 national markets. Goodman is in demand as one of the nation's foremost public speakers on streetmarketing techniques. Currently, he is the baby boom consultant for FOX Network Television. In the last five years alone, he has been the featured repeat speaker for the American Hotel and Motel Association, Hotel Sales and Marketing Association International, Independent Television, California Hotel/Motel Association, Australian Tourism Marketing Council of North America, Tourism Association of Southern California, National Association of Broadcasters, Long Beach Area Convention and Visitors Council and

Preferred Hotels and Resorts Worldwide.

When asked in an interview about why boomers refuse to emulate their parents, Goodman explained that boomers have three major concerns: providing an education for their children, caring for their aging parents and waiting for an inheritance from those parents who saved every penny for them. They don't want to be like their parents. They have no intention of waiting until retirement for a two-week cruise. In fact they are terrified of retirement and old age. They are intent on remaining teenagers until the day they die. It is only fair, then, to expect boomers to be different from generations preceding them.

This book is unique because it will fix something that is broken. Also, Goodman is not just another informed businessperson. His well-placed national electronic media contacts make him a natural promotional associate for the entire project. For five years, he has been tracking the boomer. His commitment to the "today" mentality of marketing is the thrust of his life's work. And finally, Goodman's specialized field of tourism is recognized as the barometer of the country's economic trends with regard to the boomer.

Because of the author's public profile as a respected authority on this subject, the media has long awaited this valuable work. Indications are that, because of its focus on tangible answers for concerned commercial industries, it will become a handbook for a variety of market analysts as well as consumers. Like other business handbooks of great magnitude, this work promises to be concise, quotable and immensely useful by management at any level. Like its author, it is straightforward, challenging and provocative.

BOOMERS
The Ageless Generation

Sell them if you can!

PREFACE

Little did I dream back in the '50s and '60s when I was a disc jockey in Los Angeles that the teenagers in my audience would one day be called the Baby Boom Generation and that I would be researching them. Back then, everyone thought that rock 'n' roll was a fad that would go away as fast as it came in. They didn't figure that those teenagers would bring their music and their youthful attitudes with them right into their adult world.

When I talked to my radio audiences back then, what I *did* know was that they were going to grow up to be completely different from their parents. But it wasn't until 1987 that I fully realized the power of their generation and the likely effect boomers will have on the next three decades or more.

Other books and articles written about this generation are filled with statistics. This book deals with the reality of the boomer mind-set. I know that I view the boomers from a completely different perspective from other writers and marketers. To evaluate this generation, I just used the ordinary common sense I inherited from my mother and father, who were no-nonsense people with follow-through that wouldn't quit!

Oh, sure, there will be some statistics. More than 76 million babies were born in this country between 1946 and 1964. 51% of those babies were female. 1957 was the peak year with 4.3 million babies born. Almost one-third of the United States population is comprised of boomers.

These are facts, and important ones, but sheer numbers alone don't help too much when it comes to understanding what may be the most misunderstood generation ever in this country. Tossed in for good measure, you'll find some charts and graphs to help you decode boomers and echo boomers a great deal better. All the hogwash and speculation based on those statistics and suppositions on how the boomer will be in mid-life and then senior years are what inspired me to write this book. Because I've learned to understand them, I've been able to help clients set all-time sales records. My 35 years in advertising and marketing wouldn't have been the same without the impact of the boomers. It is one thing to have the data from surveys and research, but then what do you do with it to help sell? I can help you find out — as I salute this ageless generation!

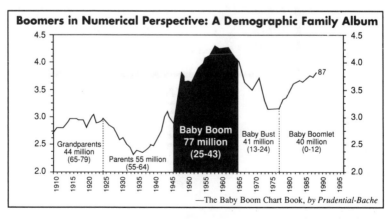

*Chart reprinted from **The Boomer Report***

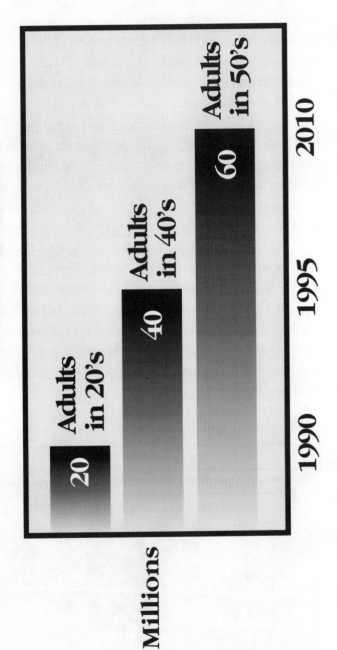

Adult Market

Adults in 20's — 20
Adults in 40's — 40
Adults in 50's — 60

Millions

1990   1995   2010

Entering Middle Age: The Boomers Turn 40

	Number of Boomers Turn 40	Boomers Aged 40 And Over
1986	2,891,000	2,891,000
1987	3,890,000	6,780,000
1988	3,655,000	10,428,000
1989	3,684,000	14,102,000
1990	3,762,000	17,846,000
1991	3,680,000	21,684,000
1992	3,795,000	25,446,000
1993	4,011,000	29,415,000
1994	4,105,000	33,469,000
1995	4,216,000	37,623,000
1996	4,257,000	41,803,000
1997	4,383,000	46,096,000
1998	4,409,000	50,397,000
1999	4,459,000	54,730,000
2000	4,527,000	59,109,000
2001	4,583,000	63,523,000
2002	4,373,000	67,702,000
2003	4,351,000	71,832,000
2004	4,303,000	75,884,000

Source: Bureau of the Census

Chart reprinted from **The Boomer Report**

Spendable Discretionary Income of Households

• The 45 to 54 age group is tricky. In 1994, boomers will be 30 to 48 years old, so the major population bulge in the 45-54 group comes from the 45-48-year-olds, not the 49-54-year-olds. This may affect what most of the increase in discretionary income is spent on.

Age	Percent of Households With Discretionary Income	Average Spendable Discretionary Income	1989 Estimated Aggregate Spendable Discretionary Income (In Billions)	1994 Projected Aggregate Spendable Discretionary Income (In Billions)	Increase (Decrease) From 1989 to 1994 (In Billions)	Percent Increase (Decrease) From 1989 to 1994
15–24	18.7%	$7,896	$43.3	$42.7	($.6)	(1.40%)
25–34	29.5%	$10,161	$192.6	$190.6	($2.0)	(1.10%)
35–44	31.8%	$13,382	$263.2	$280.6	$17.4	6.60%
45–54	32.6%	$14,189	$201.0	$241.6	$40.6	20.20%
55–64	31.9%	$14,667	$192.3	$190.7	($1.6)	(.86%)
65+	23.9%	$12,131	$247.2	$276.9	$29.6	12.00%
Total	**28.9%**	**$12,500**	**$1,139.6**	**$1,223.1**	**$83.5**	**7.33%**

Note: All dollar values are in 1989 dollars.

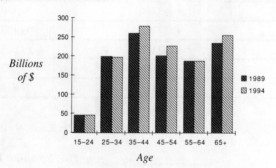

Source: From calculations by The Boomer Report and FIND/SVP, Inc. based on data from the U.S. Bureau of the Census, The Conference Board and Donnelly Demographics

Charts reprinted from **The Boomer Report**

The Boomer Report Forecast of Income and Discretionary Spending Power For 1994

Population By Age

• The 1-15 age group is projected to increase by a million people. The children and teen markets will still be kicking.

Age	1989 Estimate	1994 Projection	Increase (Decrease) from 1989 to 1994	Percent Increase (decrease) from 1989 to 1994
0–15	51,863,853	52,952,791	1,088,938	2.1%
15–24	39,906,461	38,806,842	(1,099,619)	(2.76%)
25–34	40,284,181	39,948,121	(336,060)	(.83%)
35–44	35,579,337	37,865,802	2,286,465	7.26%
45–54	25,018,142	30,006,659	4,988,517	19.94%
55–64	22,154,315	21,962,761	(191,554)	(.86%)
65+	32,037,118	35,720,272	3,683,154	11.50%
Total	**246,843,407**	**257,263,248**	**10,419,841**	**4.22%**

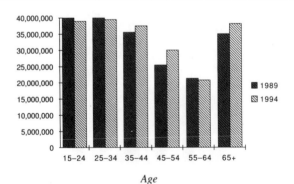

Age

Charts and graphs prepared by Hedi Katz, Statistician
Source: From calculations by The Boomer Report and FIND/SVP, Inc. based on data from the
U.S. Bureau of the Census, The Conference Board and Donnelly Demographics

CHAPTER 1

History

Where do boomers come from?

What a sad commentary on our multi-million dollar marketing industry, rife with financial wizards, that so many businesses are going broke each year by underestimating their target audience! Isn't it therefore now critical that they challenge prevailing attitudes concerning the direction of the all-important "mature money?"

I will provide the basic ideology for a total marketing strategy geared toward the business marketer who wishes to reach that economically underestimated population born between 1946 and 1964 known as THE BOOMER. I want to explore how and why our country is currently in the hands of the boomer. Anyone can write about the future and feel safe because it is not provable. But I have dealt with the economic realities of the present — what is working and what isn't and why.

What I am going to share with you is the background of the boomer and how this phenomenon evolved from 1946 to 1964, the time span generally accepted as the Baby Boom Generation. The end of World War II started the "baby boom" generation that spanned 19 years. No one really knows why the boom lasted for that period of time. All we really know is that this generation, partly because of its awesome numbers, is going to be different from any generation in the history of our country. What was to follow after 1946, no one could have predicted.

After the war, the good life set in pretty quickly. Servicemen were returned to civilian life, got married, and started raising babies. And, did they ever have a lot of kids! The impact was so great, it completely revolutionized the diaper industry. What no one knew back then was that just about every industry was going to be affected.

Attitudes changed. There was that aura of confidence that came with victory. Those who had faced death, and who realized how tenuous life could be, were determined that their children were going to have the best childhood and enjoy all the good things life has to offer. Parents wanted their children to have everything they hadn't had as children. The best education. Opportunities for travel. And great amounts of attention—some say too much attention—perhaps spoiling them rotten.

Since there were approximately 77 million boomers brought by the button-down stork in those nineteen years, it has been natural for statisticians to lump them into one group for observational purposes. Although this label makes it easier for demographics, it has no meaning for the marketer. There are really several generational levels within that time span and the effect is that there can be no set rules and no predictions about boomer behavior, except that there are no predictions!

Remember the '50s and how they were drenched in mediocrity? The flat effect of our national community reflected itself vaguely on that fandangled new invention, the television. The only element of our society more uninspiring than our beloved Ike, was the youth culture. White gloves, church socials, and saddle shoes were eventually to evolve into computer dating, women on their own and finally, this "Boomer Thing."

The early '60s became the perfect backdrop for the drama that would change the American marketplace forever. We could have done worse than to have lived then. There was a smug sense of well-being pervading every tract home nestled behind its well-manicured lawn. Sensibly-shod Mamie would soon be forever replaced by Jackie and the New Women. Treaties were being signed and unemployment was down.

There was a 4% increase in per-capita income. "Father knew best" when he advised it was prudent to accept the concept of deferred gratification. However, rapidly advancing technology, shifting political parameters, and rebellious ideology were all factors that would soon lead Americans to change their relationships with many elements of their lives, especially their money. The youth culture was truly "into themselves." The economy encouraged them to be risk-takers and leap from tall financial footings as their parents cringed in fears learned from their Depression-era parents. The entire generation of boomers is full of disparity, economic discrepancies and sociological contradictions. Some are poor, some are rich, not all are educated. But they have impacted our fiscal history simply by their numbers. Colored by the technology and politics around them, they share enough common history to make them an "intimate" generation. They are united by their disillusionment of the broken promises of postwar euphoria and pride in their rebellious political attitude. Indeed, it was a time of bitter polarization between the genders as well as generations, and a generalized battering by the advertising industry catering to their materialism. As they say, it was the worst of times and the best of times as an entire generation witnessed a major sociological upheaval unfold – one that would forever change the face of our economy, psychology and the American Dream.

On its cover, *Newsweek* labeled 1984 the "Year of the Yuppie." Even though they were essentially a small group, they were the darlings of the media. Thanks to the intense focus of their changing ways, they became enthralled with themselves as a group and began to exhibit like characteristics. They had their own dress code. They bought grown-up toys like espresso makers, pasta makers and designer watches. They believed the media about their own rampant egos and as a result, developed a work ethic of achievement and purchasing power. Their image was one of success and marketers wanted their dollars. Their self-indulgence was fodder for commercials and target marketing, and no doubt their buying habits became one of the most surveyed activities of all time.

Their influence was everywhere. They truly believed that they would always have discretionary income. They were having fun with wine and imported cheese. They ruled. For the most part, boomers enjoyed their childhoods so much, it's easy to understand why they are reluctant to grow up. The problems and challenges that faced them while they were children are problems and challenges they continue to face today, and that's part of the reason they've brought their youth culture right along with them into adulthood.

While hundreds of books and reports have documented previous generations and their potential effect on the world of their future, it seems there is considerable contradiction in trying to define the boomer generation. Some even call it an indefinable segment of the population. Are they hard to define because we still don't know who they are or where they're coming from? Is everyone afraid to try to pin the boomers down or find out what they're all about? Although, truth be told, why would it really matter why the baby boom started? It is just a matter of record. It doesn't really have anything to do with the mind-set of the boomers, and it's that mind-set that will affect every industry in this country because of the way boomers think.

I believe that the boomer has gotten some real bad raps over the years, but as I see it, the biggest problem with the entire boomer generation is that it has been tagged with the name "baby." It connotes immaturity. It is the very word "baby" that makes retailers think these "kids" aren't yet old enough to buy anything! It is the word "baby" that conjures the vision of precocious sand box executives, instead of the current and still-emerging movers and shakers. Many of them are physicians, attorneys and heads of businesses both small and large. The nation's second highest executive is a boomer—Vice-President Dan Quayle. Headlines about "The Donald," another conspicuous boomer, can't have escaped your notice. While many are still quite young, let's not forget, some of those "babies" are now viewing retirement looming on the horizon in just about twenty more years! So I am *definitely* throwing out the word "baby" in this book.

Please understand, though, that I have nothing against older people. I'm old enough myself to have two grandchildren, so I obviously have no bone to pick with the

older generation itself. We are just talking about the protocol-
itis of what is real and what isn't real. It might be ego-
gratifying to make the case that only those of us older than
fifty are worth considering when it comes to advertising and
marketing. But that flies so obviously into the face of reality
that I can't buy into the "golden-agers have all the
discretionary gold" mentality. On the other hand, I have no
gripe that I miss being included in the earliest of boomers by
just a year shy of a decade. Just having all those younger
people around is making me feel younger. Besides, my life's
work is marketing, and I want to help see that it's done right
for all age groups, even though I'll be concentrating on the
boomers.

Audiences at my speeches are amazed at how little they
know about this "boomer" thing, and thank me for the
education. After listening to me and thinking over the things
I've said, many have changed their marketing plans
completely. They've come to realize boomers won't let
themselves be mass-marketed. They agree that boomers will
be different, even when they reach their 70s. And they
absolutely understand that boomers need to be marketed as
the "young," not the aging. What appeals to today's 50-year-
olds will not appeal to boomers when they reach that age.

Because I was a disc jockey in Los Angeles in the '50s and
'60s, I can tell you that many of my teenage fans haven't
changed that much since then, and this is particularly true of
those I know from the '60s. Their basic thinking and outlook
on life have stayed pretty much the same.

What are the major trends I've noticed? I do see more
boomers becoming homebodies. They care about their
children's education. They are concerned about their aging
parents. Some boomers are returning to places of worship. A
1991 survey reported in *The Boomer Report* concerning a

survey by two church sociologists, Wade Roof and David Roozen, found "that two-thirds of the boomers left organized religion during the past few decades, but in recent years, about a third of them have returned."

Researchers found that even in the area of religion, boomers want customization. Also mentioned in the July '91 *The Boomer Report,* "But for boomers, the range of places of worship is diverse. While the 1950s saw mainline Protestants representing two-thirds of the population, today boomers are to be found in mosques and meeting halls" To paraphrase, Protestant churches want to unify; boomers want to diversify, and are therefore looking for custom-made religious beliefs. Findings from the "National Survey of Religious Identification, 1989-1990; City University of New York," are incorporated in *The Boomer Report* coverage of church-going boomers.

This book is my attempt to present an overview as to who they are and where they come from. I'll try to offer an up-to-the-minute explanation of what this generation is all about and what it's going to take to pique their interest.

There's been much said and written lately about the boomer generation entering middle age. Let's define middle age, and then let's find out what all this means to the boomer, especially the older sector of this generation. First of all, by past standards of most normal people, middle age starts at forty years of age and ends at age sixty. This may vary a few years either way. Now I challenge all the psychologists in this country to find me a 40-year-old boomer who will say he or she is middle-aged and give you a written guarantee how to market and sell him or her. Don't you get it? It is the older boomer born 1946 to 1955 that was the most radical in this generation. And in order to market and sell to them, you must realize they they are the real adult teenage population.

The younger boomers born 1956 to 1964 weren't really

caught up in all the radical movements in this country when they were teenagers. Considering that the younger boomers outnumber the older ones, let's get real and start to understand that the only thing you need to do to sell this massive segment of our population will be to throw out most marketing techniques of the past on middle age and start selling them one year at a time. I am telling you, if you try to find a regular pattern on how to market and sell to the boomer, you'll get completely blind sided.

Young boomers total more than 40% of people in professional positions and almost 37% of people in executive, managerial or administrative positions. According to sales and marketing publications, two thirds of them are earning $50,000 a year or more. Basically, boomers are the first generation that will bring their youthful society with them and they'll never really grow up. And that's great for retail sales.

Boomers are forcing us to re-examine the relationships between boss and employee. Boomers don't think much of corporate America and feel industry is not meeting the needs of its workers. Older bosses see boomers as selfish, over-indulged wastrels; boomers see their bosses as rigid and lacking in understanding of what life should really be all about. If boomers' closest friends really are their co-workers, it would be nifty to have the boss man or lady included in that professional circle of friends. Management that understands the boomers' need to enjoy their work will contribute a great deal toward a truce between them and American industry. It may be because they were the shining ones, those first post-war babies, that so much was and is expected of them. Perhaps as boomers move more and more into "bosshood," they will work better with their younger compatriots who like to have a say and who need to be challenged and appreciated for their creative input to a firm's success. Ponder this, though:

some findings reveal that boomer bosses are autocratic. Strange behavior, isn't it? Boomers experienced a level of freedom as they grew up that would have been unthinkable in the "olden days." One would have expected them to offer that latitude to their employees.

The government was trusted by boomers' parents, distrusted by boomers. The economy was a disaster while boomer parents were growing into adulthood. For boomers, the economy was a soaring success! It's such a cliche, but what influences one as a child, usually remains.

If boomers were only using wishful thinking to believe they would never grow old, and then refusing to do anything to stay young and healthy, that would indicate one heck of an unrealistic attitude. But look at how habits are changing. Membership in fitness centers has exploded. Enlightened employers are adding gyms and swimming pools to their building plans. The food industry is being revolutionized to accommodate changing tastes. Sales of *"hard liquor"* are down. According to an article in the *San Diego Union,* beer brewers are reacting to the trend by introducing non-alcoholic brews to suit this generation. Light versions of popular beer favorites are gaining in popularity. More and more boomers, partly egged on by their kids, have quit smoking. And if you think these boomer-inspired changes haven't reached all generations, wait until the next youthful-looking jogger you watch turns around to face you and you see that it's a boomer's mom or dad sporting designer sweats! Increasingly, it may even be grandma or grandpa kicking up the cinders on the jogging track. Clinging to youth, especially when it leads to a healthier lifestyle, is not a negative; it's a positive that may well lead to a better quality of life for everyone.

This book takes a look at marketers and businesses that have been dwelling on the senior citizens and their alleged "disposable income" far too long. They have been catering to the seniors but missing out on capturing the attention of the boomer. Now is the time to embrace and court the boomer, and to do that, one must understand the boomer mind-set. I hope to bring the keys to unlock that mind-set thereby allowing industries to recognize what's necessary to sway the boomer to their product or service. The boomer generation is elusive and changes with the wind, caused in large part by the influence of the events that occurred while they were going through childhood. I believe that the boomer mind-set would have been the same whether the number of babies born was almost 77 million or 57 million. It was the series of culture shocks that hit this generation during the '60s and '70s that changed this generation for life. What all this means is that marketers all over the country are going to have to sell their clients on advertising more often, and be willing to change tactics in midstream if necessary.

The real controversy of this book will hinge on marketing versus psychology. There has been a flood of articles and plenty of books written by psychologists and others attempting to explain the boomer based on past generations. This is pure folly. These experts have an alarming tendency to offer their projections as absolutes. It might be okay if they tempered their beliefs and offered them as possibilities, but so many of them make their statements as though they had been handed down to Moses on Mount Sinai! I've seen a great number of marketing and advertising plans based on these "absolutes." They've been taken as gospel, to the long-lasting detriment to advertising and marketing plans. Boomers are totally different from everyone before them, therefore they demand a fresh approach. The words "conventional" and "predictable" are not even in their vocabularies.

Because of our adherence to tradition, a common mistake

is made by experts when they look at our birthrate during the years 1965 to 1976. In that 12-year span, a birthrate dip of 10 million fewer babies occurred in this country; but when it came to predictions for what the birthrate was going to be from 1976 on, just about everyone missed the boat carrying all those little newborns! In 1984 alone, the Bureau of the Census underestimated by 14% the number of babies to be born to women aged 30 to 34; and missed it by a whopping 55% when it came to predictions for women in the 35-39-year-old group bearing children. They are continuing to miss the mark. No one expected 4.2 million new births in 1990, and this year, it looks like we'll be seeing 4.5 million in strollers and baby carriages. What does that really mean? For one thing, the American woman is changing all those predictions about an aging population. Take it from me, the young adult and children's market is very much alive and kicking!

According to professional polls, projections indicate that billions and billions of dollars will be spent by boomers alone in the year 2000. I say that this is faulty speculation. I will argue that prediction is impossible, especially since the boomer may not have much money left for discretionary spending. Somebody has to pay to feed, clothe and educate all those "unpredicted" children. The United States will be a youth culture well into our next century.

So what will happen? By the year 2000, the over-45 population will make up more than 35% of the national population and this will translate into 75 million people reaching their middle years all at once. Naturally, every marketmonger will attempt to capture their fancy. As a key focus of this book, I will be questioning the wisdom of basing economic decisions on traditional past generational performance. Statistics provided by leading data research centers such as FIND/SVP demonstrate that understanding the boomer as a consumer is one of the most urgent economic concerns of the worried purveyors of commerce. They are looking for answers right now in the '90s. They face a crucial need to be able to formulate the methods necessary to go after their target population.

If all the psychology and trend forecasting books were effective, why is everyone still struggling to find the appropriate means of reaching and understanding the boomer? I'll tell you why. It is because the majority of people who read those books and articles really don't believe them. Psychology can't predict the future, no matter how many learned experts are quoted or how long one may have worked with a certain segment of the population.

Yet while offering up findings and possible solutions to the understanding of the boomer, you may come up with conclusions of your own. After all, this is an ongoing study and the boomer is still young, still unpredictable and still as exciting as ever. So now is the time to break away from the study of historical generations and acquaint ourselves with the generation of today—the boomer generation.

Let's take a look at how the almost 77 million boomers (4.3 million born in 1957 alone) and their children in this country are categorized. 51% are female; 49% are male. Boomers comprise the first major population where the gender ratio did a flip-flop and females became the majority. There are two distinct boomer groups—those age 27 to 35, and the older boomers, age 36 to 45. "Echo Boomers," boomers' children, now tagged with their own identifying moniker, also enter the equation in a way bigger than and different from the way youngsters have ever impacted markets in the past. Older boomers are the more radical of the boomers, and feel and act more like teenagers than the younger boomers do. They grew up in the '60s, the most radical period in our country's history, and came out of that decade during their teens and early twenties. They emerged from those troubled years scarred by events that left indelible marks on all of us.

I don't see why people find it so hard to accept the mind-set of any generation and realize that social conditions in our country set the tone for the rest of our lives, from birth to the end. And when one considers the world situation faced by the first wave of boomers, it's easy to prove the point.

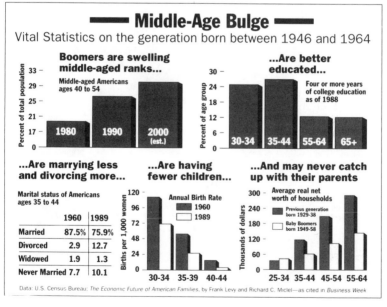

*Chart reprinted from **The Boomer Report***

CHAPTER 2

Marketing vs. Psychology

Sell them,
don't tell them!

As this marketing mystery of "who is buying what and why" has unfolded over the last several years, a plethora of psycho-social statistics has been put forth to explain the cause and impact of the boomers' buying mystique. But, until now, no one has actually provided solid, workable tactics to manage this economic phenomenon of the generation that refuses to grow up or old.

A new strategy must appeal moment to moment, not year to year. The manner in which this demographic bulge developed and, more importantly, how it is affecting today's marketplace is the key to my method of identifying and managing the target, that elusive boomer!

We must forever dispel the myth of mass-marketing the boomer! For example, unlike their parents, they have no product loyalty. Also unlike their parents, their consumer spending accounts for the largest share of the gross national product. Reports show that although the boomers may be less interested than their parents in spending for essentials such as food and shelter, their discretionary expenditures are on the upward climb. To be sure, this age group is driven toward consumption of luxury products and services.

Remember, the first rule is that there are no rules. So, appeal to their intelligence level. Appeal to their impulsive nature. Offer them tremendous bargains on a limited time basis. Appeal to their children definitely. Appeal to their reasoning or lack of it.

A term coming into wider and wider use to describe older boomers is "the sandwich generation." Boomers are depicted as feeling the pressure from aging, and possibly ill parents from above, and the demands made upon them by their school-age children from below. I'll be discussing these pressures in the chapters that follow.

My many years in radio and other media have given me a hands-on approach which has enabled me to separate fact from fiction regarding marketing the boomer. When I say, "40-year olds aren't having a mid-life crisis," I know why--and the economic impact of this statement! I believe that the boomers experienced their crises in youth, as opposed to mid-life as predicted by psychologists. My findings are backed by the University of California survey in which 300 boomers of various occupations, indicated that their crises came in childhood and high school. They haven't felt anything resembling a mid-life crisis as they approach or reach 40.

Also, in a 1991 Gallup Poll, older boomers were asked if

they had been through a mid-life crisis. In response, 69% said "no", 27% said "yes" and 4% had "no opinion." This phenomenon and its ramifications are at the center of my challenge of the myths and conventional wisdom of this group.

True, my attempt to define boomers and hold their attention long enough to close them is not based on scientific samplings. In fact, I don't even claim to be objective. My findings and evaluations are not based on subjective theory either. I know these people and find them to be the most complex, diverse, and economically puzzling generation in the history of sales.

The whole point of addressing their generational discrepancies is to emphasize the urgent need to change the method of reaching the marketers' target. Boomers' process of "growing up," if they have one, is haphazard. They cannot be plagued by the trappings of the traditional American adult agenda. For example, how will they have a marital crisis if they can't decide to marry? How will they have a job crisis if they still haven't found the right job by mid-years? Why should they worry and save for the mortgage when they can't afford a house in the first place? Contrary to the "experts," I believe that the economy has created this mind-set. Since only 5% of the national population currently makes more than $100,000, and since that same 5% has remained steady over time, how can we blame consumerism and economic disasters on the boomers? They are therefore, as consumers, victims of their own internal contradictions. Our financial ideology may have spawned their development, but the potentially dangerous trends we are facing were not planted by their generation. But watch them sprout there.

This work is intended to catapult the mental giants of marketing directly into the present decade. I will prove that, along with the departure of so many generational mores, gone also are the time-honored myths of market strategy. In my own rhetoric, I will prove that indeed gone are the rules and righteous ramblings of the revered past! Since the advent of walking upright, each generation has taken a condescending attitude toward the previous generation, viewing them as somehow socially inferior, thereby assuring their own superiority. Not so anymore. At some point in the '50s, something happened.

Psychologists and other experts have been running amuck and falling all over themselves trying to predict and contradict each other about future boomer behavior. As the prime example of how inexact such forecasting can be, predictions made in 1932 in Aldous Huxley's <u>Brave New World</u>, and those taken as gospel in 1949 when George Orwell penned <u>1984</u>, just haven't come to be. And those two who missed the mark are just among the more noted and quoted of the predictors of the not-so-distant past. They were precursors of the current crop of experts who continue to miss the boomer target when they shoot the prediction arrows into the atmosphere as they conjecture boomers' behavior by looking into the past to see what others did as they grew older.

Current books discussing demographics affecting banking, business and government had their leaders tripping over each other to hail these works as sources of major revelations. Some of these writers fail to recognize the boomer as a different breed of cat. They fail to perceive that boomers should be the main focus now.

All one has to do is look at the business pages of any newspaper to note that it's the formation and growth of industries that cater to the entrepreneurial spirit of boomers and new hi-tech industries that are currently making their mark and moving our country forward.

These writers presume that America has a romance with the aging process. Like other lesser commentaries on the subject, these works would have us believe that youth is soon to be happily overcome by the militant gray panther mentality which has accepted age gracefully. Although these writers have probed the workings of the boomer mind, the complex potential and financial fallout are best left to the street marketers like myself.

In spite of all the ambitious academia involved in the study of the trends of generations, the conclusions can only be speculation. I challenge their conclusions and then take the matter several steps from there! I can help you translate their intricate pop psychology into dollars for our sagging economy.

Some experts speak about the care-giver generation, and envision a world where the elderly will continue to receive their care primarily from women. They appear to make the assumption that today's boomer will do nothing to change the current social system, and thus will accept the current care-giving role without question and without change. Can you see this actually happening? Boomers have the money and the technology to free themselves for leisure and personal pursuits and provide even better care for their aging parents.

Troubling signs on the care horizon do exist, however. Contrary to popular belief, most nurses are boomers born during the early stages of the boom and many of them have children that need care after the school day ends. The most serious "illness" facing the health care industry is the critical shortage of skilled nurses. The medicine to solve this shortage is a bitter pill for hospitals and other care facilities to swallow. Better salaries, more flexibility in work hours, on-site day care centers for children, and perhaps even for the elderly—all of those things and more go into the package needed to attract and keep nurses. Come to think of it, those are some of the benefits that attract workers in any field.

A marvelous opportunity exists for those who come up with creative answers to the problem of care for boomers' parents, a service many believe will overshadow the need for child care. I believe boomers will solve this two-pronged problem. They are interested in the quality of life, for their parents, children and themselves, and they aren't about to let themselves be victimized by circumstances just because they're already in place. Watch for innovations in the health care industry that will affect all of us. We'll now be concentrating of what people need and want, not on what they fear.

To help make the case that the aging population should be considered of prime importance, current experts state the obvious fact that half of the nation's millionaires are older than 65 — but they leave unsaid the fact that the other half is *younger* than 65. I find it hard not to laugh out loud. No matter who holds the wealth at the moment, boomers will be the inheritors of the older half's millions, and that will spur the economy. Other assets currently held by older Americans are going to be left to boomers as well. I'll discuss this further in the chapter on money.

Another key element in addressing this group is better understanding of the stages and gender factor of boomerhood. Do not make the mistake today of marketing to that upper echelon the way you would have 20 years ago to a population of the same age. Remember that there are four different classifications in the boomer generation based on birth years, and even though they have similarities in nature, they have to be dealt with differently because of our sociological experimentation of each particular ensuing group.

For example, in the '50s and '60s, the parental world focused on the every whim of the boomer. We created new systems of educating the "special ones," built suburbs with wet bars and hot tubs and indulged their need for that elusive phantasm known as fitness. Today, every successful marketer wants to key into the mind of these 40-year-olds who have the energy, attention span and whims of teenagers. They are the entitled ones. And their expectations of each other and certainly of their consumer products often exceed reality.

One of the main reasons I have written this book on what I call "street level" is so that I can really zero in on the mind-set of this generation and, in addition, counteract the erroneous beliefs that are being accepted. Many industries in this country are confused on how to reach the boomer. And to a great extent, that confusion has arisen because of certain books and articles written about the boomer that give mixed and contradictory signals about the very group these experts are trying to analyze.

Most boomers I talk to don't agree on what is being written about them by psychologists, forecasters and trend setters. The feel they are misunderstood by those writers and consider some of their findings as a joke or a form of fortune telling. They also feel the survey companies are way off. Boomers themselves don't share an absolute, universal view of themselves. At the same time, they certainly don't buy into any pop psychologist's evaluation that the boomers are a generation positively headed for destruction and chaos.

Boomers make fast decisions and generally resent authority. However, most of them are willing to tolerate authority in the workplace because they like the money and are determined to work and play hard. They see themselves as totally different individuals, even from their own friends and business associates. Most stories in magazines and newspapers only discuss what are the perceived similarities.

The boomers got bored over the years watching their parents buying the same products and going on the same vacations in the same places year after year. They were determined to be different when they became adults. So, among the things boomers don't share with their parents are brand loyalty and an inclination to stick with just one political party because of some unquestioning faith in the system. More about this is my chapter about boomer politics.

Retailers need to zero in on the mind-set of the boomer generation today. When you deal with the boomer generation, you deal with a mind-set of psychographics, not demographics. It drives me right up a wall when learned academic writers throw around words we don't use every day and then forget to define them and the way they're using them in this study or that. I don't want to fall into that snare, so the following are definitions of words as I'm using them in this book. Both come from <u>Webster's Third New International Dictionary.</u>

Demography / Demographics: The statistical study of the characteristics of human populations especially with reference to size and density, growth, distribution, migration, and vital statistics and the effect of all these on social and economic conditions. Psychography / Psychographics: The description of an individual's mental characteristics and their development.

To make the concept of psychographics easier to understand, just think of persons and the situation of their lives, rather than just their age or the amount of money earned or where they happen to live. For example, someone of a certain age who is married with a couple of children is very different from a person of that same age who is single. Interests of single women and men are different, even if they've used up the same number of birthday candles over their lives. Those are just a few of the things marketers and advertisers need to consider when targeting to specific audiences.

Advertising and marketing professionals and the lay public alike recognize and respect the name J. Walter Thompson, which is, to some, THE advertising agency. In 1989, JWT released a major study that combined the best of the psychographic and demographic worlds. I've certainly been in agreement with the words JWT's consumer behavior department highlighted in that study: "Age alone will become an obsolete marketing concept." Hear, hear! Where in the past marketers concentrated on groups of people by categorizing them into age, race, geographical location, education and income, for example, the tendency now is to redefine the slots into which people fit more precisely.

The October 1989 issue of *The Boomer Report* published the full results of the study, "The American Lifestages" study segments consumers by the major watershed events that determine how we live our lives.
These landmarks include:
- moving away from home
- marriage
- childbearing
- children leaving home
- divorce

Bravo to JWT for pointing out the significant differences that exist even among those who might share some of the very same basic characteristics. To help marketers target their audiences to an even more precise extent, I quote from the report: ". . . JWT has broken down the three major lifestyle segments—singles, couples and parents—into nine specific groups."

Boomers fall into the first seven segments.

- At-home Singles
- Starting-Out Singles
- Mature Singles
- Young Couples
- Young Parents
- Mature Parents
- Single Parents
- Empty Nesters
- Left-Alone Singles

JWT Uses LifeStages Not Ages To Target Boomer Markets

Boomer LifeStages in 1989	Mean Age	Size in Millions	% of Adults	Income Share In Billions ($)	Mean Personal/Household Income
At-home Singles	22	23	14	179	7,913
Starting-Out Singles	26	7	4	117	17,829
Young Couples	29	11	7	195	37,213
Young Parents	32	29	17	478	35,434
Single Parents	41	12	7	157	20,027
Mature Singles	45	8	5	165	20,713
Mature Parents	47	33	20	650	45,460

*Chart reprinted from **The Boomer Report***

Within the categories above are even further refinements. When the study was done, two-thirds of the at-home singles were working, one-third were in school. The main products they bought were listed as sporting equipment, casual clothes and personal care products. Group number two, the starting-out singles, were shown to be financially independent, but often living in multiple person households. You figured it out—this group is a heavy buyer of furniture. Mature singles were the travelers, indifferent to careers and fads. This group is a bit on the outside looking in at their peers who are married and leading active family lives. Young couples generally meant a pair of income-earners, and while they spend whopping amounts, there was a shift toward home and furniture buying. We all know where the money went for the following segment—young parents. Kids get the biggest slice of this, an often two-paycheck family. Lack of time and strains on financial resources are highlighted for this group. Mature parents were beginning to feel some relief as their offspring finished college and went out on their own, but for some, second mortgages were creating a financial pain. Single parents present the greatest mixed bag to marketers. Their product purchases are more than a bit erratic and strangely mixed. Single parents, a harried majority of whom are divorced women, bought a lot of baby food, but also were in the checkout lines to pay for cigarettes and alcohol.

The scope of this study is so deep and wide, it will serve as the Bible to marketers for years to come as they attempt to define, redefine, refine and reflect. I absolutely see it as a template for marketing success well into the future. When one combines information gleaned from this study with some street marketing smarts, failure has to be an accident! True, no study can take into consideration the differences that make each one of us unique, but as a guideline, I know of nothing better in existence. Sure, continue to use your age ranges, lists of special interest consumers, census data, and the like. But for a one-two marketing punch, the intelligent marriage of psychographics and demographics will just about guarantee that you'll hit the heights.

One of the two main myths is the lack of consensus that ours is not a youth-oriented society. Now when they talk about a youth-oriented society, sometimes you will hear psychologists lecture and you'll read or hear about the books they've written telling about the aging of the population. I have heard some say "you were born with youth being the hero, you will die with seniors being in charge." What's so loony tune about that is the fact the United States ranks eighteenth in world population of those older than 65. We don't need ANYONE to tell us that as individuals we start getting older from the minute we are born. What we do need is the recognition that among other countries of the world, the U. S. of A. has a young population. What's even more meaningful, we still have a young attitude.

John Naisbitt and his wife, Patricia Aburdene, authors of *Megatrends 2000,* have some fascinating things to say about the alleged "graying" of the population. Paraphrased from an interview by Adele Malott in *Friendly Exchange,* these respected trendcasters see our population becoming more youthful, not less, when compared to other industrialized nations. This is partly due to our country's less restrictive barriers on immigration. Malott writes, "Another great strength of the United States, Naisbitt says, is the way we 'rejuvenate and enrich our talent pool.' He points out that every year since 1970, the United States has allowed more legal immigration than the rest of the world combined, giving our population more youth and energy."

London's staid *The Economist* called U.S. marketers to task for assuming boomer families will become just like families that preceded them—"This is plainly wrong." Its March 3, '91, article cautioned against sticking with "woefully out of date" techniques based on "traditional Walton-like families of the past." To that, I say Amen!

You will see the articles or hear the speeches about the aging of the population, and how by the year 2000 there will be hundreds of millions of dollars less in income spent by those then 18-to-34-years-old, and how the boomers all the way through their senior years will be spending hundreds of millions of more retail dollars. There are two primary things wrong with those assumptions. There is only an eleven year dip in population in the boomer generation, and that was from 1965 to 1976. There were ten million fewer babies born in this country, but current figures show birthrate again going up. The problem with buying the idea that's it's smart to put all your marketing eggs into the senior market is that the year 2000 is still nine years in the future! So if marketers want to concentrate on the older audience now, it won't mean anything to the long-range success of their businesses. The key to successful marketing, as I see it, is to realize that every age group is seeing itself as younger than it actually is. Except for some kids, who think they'll never be grown-up, just about everyone else should be treated as though their outlook and attitude is young. This doesn't mean agencies should be obsessed with young, they should just recognize that by aiming young they'll cover all the marketing bases.

The September '91 issue of *Working Woman* makes some pointed observations. Debra Kent's article, "Beyond Thirtysomething," discusses the boomers' desire to fight aging "every step of the way," as depicted in easily recognizable television commercials. In ads, boomers will "want models they can relate to. Those models will have to look attractive, even if they are older." She writes, "A generation that dreads growing old is even less enthusiastic about the prospect of getting sick." She comments on the very positive interest in maintaining good health, and expects that interest will prod the medical community into making strides towards relieving and / or curing ailments of old age.

If the fact boomers want to stay young-looking leads to medical advances, I can live with that kind of result, can't you?

On the humorous side of this wanting to stay young mystique, *The San Diego Daily Transcript* ran a piece about M.G. Lord's Prig Tales: Your Guide to Surviving the Self-Righteous Nineties. The author is quoted, "A lot of kids are making fun of their parents and the fact that parents have given up alcohol and cigarettes. One kid I interviewed even said he wakes up and purposely has a Camel non-filter while dad is on the floor doing his exercises. When the boomers' kids come of age, the boomers are in big trouble." Maybe so. But I'm betting most of them will benefit from having healthy parents with young attitudes.

Marketers also are buying into the idea that boomers don't have any money to spend. Talk about goofy assumptions guaranteed to lead to market share loss! As I reported in *Business Press of Las Vegas* - I believe the revolution has just begun. Businesses that don't bring themselves up to date with reality will be left behind in reaching the most misunderstood generation in our history.

We can only hope Detroit finally learns a lesson. There's no question it lost the boomer market to foreign imports. Looks to me like the next generation of car buyers will also be facing east when it comes time to purchase wheels (unless it's affluent enough to face BMW land). Marketers have missed the boat, or should I say, missed the car, by not zooming in on the boomer and the post-boomer automobile buyer. United States cars are certainly as good as the foreign imports. Manufacturers should be going after every potential buyer they can to try to make up for lost time.

Advertising Age came up with some interesting conclusions concerning the aging of the boomer, and its effect on certain industries. One of the researchers quoted in the series mentioned there would be growth in "cosmetics, the leisure travel industry, health care and entertainment, to name a few." It was also noted, "several factors, however, complicate the once neat correlation between age and consumer behavior." In spite of the fact that it's been validated by many researchers that "this generation, more than any other generation, tends to hang onto the values and attitudes of its youth," running-scared industries are planning to change their approaches now for future years when boomers MAYBE will change product use. Even with the facts staring them right in the face, marketers insist on aiming for the boomers THEN instead of NOW. Even when it's shown boomers have a strong desire to stay young in attitude, and although it's been shown even their snacking habits are not changing significantly, it's off to la-la land for the advertisers who are right in step with those who say concentrate on the boomers tomorrow, and right out of step with boomers in today's parade.

Get with the boomers of this generation now, before it's you who are misunderstood by them. Don't let your ad dollars go down the drain of poor planning and worse comprehension.

Peering into a crystal ball isn't going to reveal a whole lot, but if you open your eyes and look around you, you'll see three areas that boomers have fostered and will continue to support. They are interested in protecting the environment, care about all areas of health and healthy living, and as more and more become parents, they are searching for ways to provide a safe setting for little Jennifer and Jeremy. Note the growth of radon detection firms and companies that specialize in turning garages into safe storage areas for hazardous items and materials.

Products that are kind to the waistline or gentle on the environment continue to see their profits heading into the stratosphere. Sales of walking shoes may be inching ahead of jogging shoes. Who cares? Boomers are the customers for both!

Opportunities abound in franchising, an ideal way to be an entrepreneur within a structure that gives advice and support over the rough spots, but leaves enough slack for individual creativity and control. In recent years, healthful food franchises have "chomped" away at fast-food mainstays. A few years ago, who would have predicted salad bars cutting in to the burger and fries market? Could you have guessed that boomers, the consummate consumers, would be asking, make that demanding, that containers be recyclable?

I read articles about the boomers changing their lives from the "me generation" to the "we generation." I read that they are spending less money as they get older and are changing their taste and buying cheaper things. I hear they are saving more money. I read about them being more concerned about their senior years. I keep seeing magazine and newspaper articles advising preparation for the senior world now as the boomer ages. They say that boomers will spend more money in their senior life because of the size of the population. They also say the post-boomer generation will have less to spend because there are fewer of them than there are in the current boomer generation. Do you know what I say about all of this? **PROVE IT!**

I haven't seen any of this come true so far in the past five to six years that I've been doing research on them. I've been tuning into their world on a street level. By that I mean by living and working with them personally on a day-to-day basis. I feel that the real truth based on case histories is more important than a bunch of statistics and quotes from a hundred different articles that basically all look alike.

Unfortunately for American business, too many marketing "experts" have been myopic in their economic evaluation of this key group. They have failed to grasp the theory that for the boomer customer, adolescence is a lifestyle rather than a stage. In attempting to apply outdated generational rules to this idiosyncratic group, economists have affected potential business growth. What is happening to them right now is key to their daring capture. Boomers, the Ageless Generation, challenges other writers in their pseudo-sophisticated evaluations.

By the simple observation of our current fiscal trends, it is obvious that this is the optimal time for economists to take a closer look at the reasons for the current trends on the charts. If an industry doesn't understand who their potential consumers are, it doesn't matter what their product is — they are not going to reach them! The wisdom of my work is not based on demographics and psychological statistics outlining how boomers should behave. I have a realistic view of them as they see themselves on the "street" day-to-day.

MARKETING CANNOT BE TAUGHT,
IT HAS TO BE DISCOVERED!

To me, it doesn't seem like an oversimplification to state boomers will consider themselves forever young. While it won't actually be a teenager's face staring back from a 45-year-old boomer's mirror; in that boomer's mind's eye, the reflection will be of someone barely post-adolescent. Sure, considering oneself younger than actual years isn't new or particularly mind-boggling. It's just that this generation, more than any other, will see itself as perennially youthful. Even when they become "senior citizens," they won't see themselves as such, and they are going to be nothing like the oldsters of today. Let me insert an important word of caution right now. If you plan to call boomers seniors as they enter those "golden ages," watch out! It's my strong belief boomers will resent, as many of today's older Americans already do, being called "seniors." When they enter their sunset years, I'll wager they'll still watch and read what they want to, even if the appeal seems to be more appropriate for the teenager market. Boomers see their financial and personal accomplishments as much more important than their chronological age, and they'll keep that belief forever.

Consider what follows a case in point. In a summer '91 *Wall Street Journal* article, it was pointed out, "Reading glasses get a makeover as they become a baby-boom accessory." Those dull-looking non-prescription glasses one can pick up in the neighborhood drugstore aren't what they used to be, and if you check the catalogs stuffing your mailbox, you'll see those aids to aging eyes now as hot items increasingly sporting a youthful fashion look. The trend to look young has spilled over into the bifocal market, as more and more designers enter the market to help disguise the fact that time is inexorably marching on, even for the boomer.

CHAPTER 3

Media

You stand a chance of going down the tubes if you don't use radio!

If all you marketing and advertising experts out there read and act on the sentence you just read in this book, that alone will make it worth the price! That advice may look simple and sound simple, and it is—if you listen up and pay attention. And take action to use radio in your advertising campaigns and marketing strategies.

A young Italian genius couldn't have fully realized what he was starting when at the boomer age of 35, about ten years after he started his telegraph company, he won a Nobel Prize in 1909 for his work on wireless transmission. But Guglielmo Marconi would probably approve of what has become of his invention. The entrepreneurial spirit he demonstrated can be reclaimed by the enlightened radio pioneers of today. Marconi "stood on the shoulders of giants" like Hertz, Maxwell and Faraday. Today's marketers can climb to new marketing heights with radio's help.

In my years of experience, NO medium has brought me and my clients the results and paid for itself over and over again more effectively, more quickly and more remarkably than radio, the most overlooked weapon in today's marketing arsenal.

It's true, those of us who huddled around the "Box"—the one without the pictures—may recall with nostalgia, programs like *The Lone Ranger, The Shadow* or *Amos and Andy,* and think radio days are gone forever. For some couch potatoes, radio has passed out of their lives just as those programs have. But radio is not *less* of an influence on the boomers than it was on us older folks. In fact, it's becoming *more!!* Boomers, mislabeled the "TV Generation," were chronologically raised with radio. Music radio was the unifying cultural force. I've noted that psychologists don't begin to comprehend the effect of entertainment on one's later life. What boomers heard growing up will remain with them forever. When boomers hear Elvis or The Supremes, they're teenagers again, no matter what their age. TV was associated with anxiety-provoking events like assassinations and the Vietnam war, not exactly happy memories to carry around for a lifetime. Add to those troubles the riots on campuses all over the country, the Hippie movement, the "Love" generation and Woodstock, and what you get is a discontented generation with tastes and interests so wide and varied that it's impossible to pigeonhole them into one group for marketing.

Heavy newspaper saturation has declined because boomers, unlike their parents and grandparents, don't read newspapers just to pass the time. They don't read the with the same leisurely attitude because of their hurried lifestyles — and because they get most of their news from TV and radio. A good example of this can be taken from Dan Cotter, marketing manager for the *St. Louis Post Dispatch*. If someone reaches age 18 and isn't reading a paper four times a week, there's only a 33% chance of converting them to a regular reader. And if a person gets to 30 without having the newspaper habit, the research shows there's only a miniscule 5% chance of turning them into a reader. Newspapers all over the country need to pay enough attention to the younger generation.

The October 14, '91 issue of *Advertising Age,* also addresses this print media situation as boomer-related. Christy Fisher's article on the evolutionary downward spiral of newspaper revenue quotes analyst Kenneth Berents, "Of the potential pool of 24 million baby boomers age 30 and older in the 1980s, only 500,000 have become newspaper subscribers. Newspapers have to change to bring in the baby-boom generation. We may look back on the '80s and realize that they were the golden period of newspapers." Moral of the story–boomers want hard-edge news that relates to them and they want it immediately. Do not assume that boomers will follow in their parents' footsteps as regular readers.

Sales of books are up, admittedly, but it's the non-fiction market that's expanding. That indicates boomers read mostly for information in areas of interest to them. Some of the giant newspaper chains are finally picking up on boomer reading habits, or should I say, non-reading habits. The birth of *USA Today* is an example of the boomer mentality to scan the universe and read what catches their eye. As evidence, who hasn't noticed the trend towards shorter stories accompanied by graphics and photos? I don't want to see newspapers disappear, but after some 35 years in advertising and marketing, I don't feel I am going out on a limb when I notice that newspapers do not have the strength they once had in this country. They will remain strong, but will never be as influential as they were in the past.

Only "niche" magazines are gaining new subscribers. It's difficult for general readership magazines to hold the attention of this hurried audience unless they cater to a particular boomer interest. In that case, publishing success is almost assured throughout this decade. If handled correctly and personalized, direct mail will have some effect because targeted mailing lists do zero in on appropriate potential respondents, but response rates rarely exceed 3 %—not a great return on an expensive investment. Junk mail is a waste of effort and postage.

Outdoor advertising, when combined with radio, makes for a good media mix. Today, when there are so many ways to get entertainment and news, it's not surprising that among the 27 to 45-year-olds, network television viewing is still falling. I have found it impossible to categorize the television viewing habits of the 76.5 million boomers. With a group that large, there is no one set of "habits" to identify. What I have learned is that only about 25 million boomers are regular viewers, and to the dismay of advertisers, those viewers constitute a downscale audience. Advertisers and programmers are in a quandary about getting a desirable audience in front of the set. The only television audience that has been increasing in the past twenty-five years is the audience comprised of those older than 50. Why networks are concentrating on an audience that doesn't spend and ignoring the boomer potential audience that does, is one of life's great mysteries to me. To bring boomers into the viewing fold is going to take a lot of work, and so far, it seems only FOX Network and some of the independent cable stations have come upon the winning combination of appealing savvy.

Easily accessed entertainment is important, especially for those boomers who work in stressful pressure cooker jobs. Boomers turn to their VCRs or compact disc players to relieve the cares of the day. To a great extent, the boomers' harried lifestyle is of their own doing because they are creating some of the pressures themselves by being so fiercely competitive. The death knell hasn't sounded for any single component of the media, but to capture the boomer, media must make significant changes to tune in to their mind-set.

Here I offer a suggestion. If you have already captured the boomer viewer, especially on any of the independent cable stations, stick with the format. Boomers like specialization and will switch faster than a New York minute if stations start to offer a mix they don't want or appreciate.

It's time for a little bedtime story kind of a "once upon a time" parable that proves a lot of my points. Quoting from my "Guerrilla Marketing" column in *The Boomer Report* of June 15, '91: From sign-on to sign-off, KGUN-TV is number one with the 18 to 49-year-old market. So where is this top-rated boomer station? In some Thirtysomething mecca like Philadelphia? Wrong. KGUN is in Tucson, Arizona—a retirement haven for senior citizen "snow birds" fleeing from northern climes.

So KGUN must rate dead last with these 50+ gray panthers, right? Wrong again. KGUN is first with both boomers and retirees. Listen up, class. When planning your programming, your advertising campaigns, your media buys, your marketing strategies—aim at the boomers—and the seniors will follow.

KGUN station manager, Jim Thompson, is reaping the benefits of that network's decision to program for the younger audience in spite of "expert" observations that seniors are the spenders. Jim believes it would be futile to chase after the senior market when boomers are doing the larger share of spending on retail products. He holds the view that while seniors may have more discretionary income, they cling to depression-era spending habits and aren't as likely to purchase the products advertised.

The process of switching around programs so that one never knows when they're going to be telecast is something Thompson has learned is a real turn-off to the short-of-time boomers. To the extent possible, he keeps a dependable program schedule. Seniors may have the time and make the effort to track down their favorite shows. Boomers won't. They'll substitute something else for entertainment, and zap, there goes an entire viewing family. In this era of diminishing television viewing, no TV manager wants to subtract from his already dwindling audience and encourage station viewers to pop a movie with no commercials into the VCR.

Selling ads for Thompson's station is made easier because his account executives can show what is in actuality three viewing audiences—boomers, their children, and the senior citizens. Once again—go for the boomers and the seniors will follow!

Let me share with you some other excerpts from my "Guerrilla Marketing" columns. These appeared in *The Boomer Report* July 15, '91 and August 15, '91 issues. Awhile back, I approached an executive from FOX Broadcasting Company to learn firsthand why the network was changing its approach and zeroing in on the boomer market when almost everyone else appeared to be concentrating on the older viewer. I learned they were following a successful pattern adopted by ABC, when in the '70s, it went after young audiences. Sad to say, ABC did not stick to its original strategy, and now is again losing market share. FOX doesn't want to make that mistake. When it learned it was holding first place among child and teen viewers in the early afternoon and evening, it capitalized on that knowledge. It started to offer programs in prime time that would continue to hold that audience and pull in mom and dad. FOX realized that kids and teens make a great number of decisions concerning what the entire family is going to watch.

It hasn't hurt FOX at all to be perceived as different from the other networks, more risk-taking, more exciting, and a great deal less of a copy cat. Lo and behold, with *The Simpsons,* FOX captures both boomers and echo boomers— viewers aged 2 to 49! And advertisers love having that kiddie audience. FOX is planning to keep its successful shows, but at the same time it will take daring plunges to offer new and different ones. While it absolutely will give new shows a chance to catch on, watch for frequent additions to the FOX line-up to take advantage of boomers' desire for the new. We'll all be watching to see how the FOX scheduling succeeds.

I am serving as a consultant to FOX Network, and have been working on a series of focus group surveys around the country. My job is to interpret the answers to questions we ask, but perhaps more importantly, we'll be working together to learn how well the questions are comprehended by boomer groups. What FOX and I hope to accomplish is to learn what boomers are thinking about and what they think of themselves. It's a definite exercise of applied street level marketing. The results will provide a golden opportunity for all marketing planners and for the media.

Andy Fessel, senior vice-president of research for the FOX Network, has been kind enough to share some of his observations with me that I will paraphrase as follows. Although the demographics of boomers of all ages (27 to 45 years old) are important, FOX Network may not be inclined to follow all boomers as they age. Rather, they are planning their programming primarily to appeal to a younger age group, those now 12 to 34-years-old, which encompasses the younger boomers born in and after 1957, and the echo boomers. The strategy is to invest and then reinvest with that crowd by renewing programs popular with them, and by adding new programs that appeal directly and strongly to those age groups. MTV has clearly taken that approach. It has let the audience that grew up with it go to VH-1 while continuing to concentrate on attracting younger viewers to hold a steady audience base.

The average age of FOX viewers has been 28, close to the low end of the boomer generation. In the five years that FOX has been in existence, they haven't seen a significant change in the age of most of their viewers. It continues to hover around those in their mid-to-late twenties. Their initial appeal was to the younger viewer, and they believe it is important to stay focused on those viewers.

Fessel continued that they have proven this with the success of *21 Jump Street,* that appealed to males from 18 to 34, and some female viewers as well. *Married with Children* is a strong boomer show, and they planned for it to be broadcast on Sunday evenings when members of a boomer household are most likely to watch it together. *The Tracy Ullman Show* was probably the quintessential boomer/yuppie show.

When they made the choice to think young, however, they didn't want to neglect older viewers completely. That's why FOX continued with a couple of shows, such as *America's Most Wanted,* watched avidly by adults from age 35 to 54. But research has shown them that they rarely attract the 50+ audience. "It is amazing", says Fessel. "It's like someone closes the door after a certain age. We don't intentionally close that door to the older viewer, but because we do focus on the young, their habits, and lifestyles, the older viewer is not as likely to watch our shows."

Perhaps it is because anyone born before the television revolution in the early '50s uses television differently and has established habits. Clearly the boomers and echo boomers, who grew up with the technological explosion, are more apt to experiment and try different things. They have amazing television savvy and know what they want of the television industry. They use the new technology—their VCRs, their remote controls and cable TV—they even shift time to suit their schedules by recording favorite programs.

Fessel thinks boomers found FOX Network and latched onto it as they were selecting from an expanding menu of programs on independent channels. Boomers are all over the channels and haven't stuck with a few favorites as the older population does. Boomers respond well to promotions that have themes and messages appropriate to their lifestyles.

FOX Network has become part of boomer households where very often children and teens introduce programs to their parents. In some families, the teenagers are watching FOX while their parents do something else. In some households, it's the case of parent and children watching the same show on separate television sets, but there are also shows that bring the entire family together, and FOX does extraordinarily well with larger families. They have benefited from this approach to program over time for the entire young household. When the youngsters watch, they get the parents to sample the shows. When shows appeal to parents, they get the kids to join them in watching. And the parents have really appreciated the children's network.

By trying different ways, times and formats, FOX is trying to get into the entire household, and by expanding to present news programs, sports, specials and programs geared to children, teens, young and middle-age adults, they are becoming more and more effective.

"We used focus study groups to work with Phil in some initial research on boomers. From them, we learned about the differences and similarities of their viewing habits and that of their parents," said Fessel. "Perhaps the major difference between these groups is the size of the television universe that they view, think about and use. Younger people are including a wider variety on their viewing menu. They mention CNN, ESPN and Discovery as part of their individual mix, their viewing diet.

"Although different age groups use the medium for different reasons, all groups want entertainment and information to help them escape the cares of the day. Older boomers are dealing with the new responsibilities they have as they become parents themselves. It's difficult to project what direction the network will move toward far into the future. There is, however, a noticeable hunger on the part of boomers for something new and different, in addition to a real appreciation of some of the existing comedy, reality shows and variety programs, like those mentioned and *In Living Color, The Ultimate Challenge, Greatest Stunts* and *Cops.*

Those who took part in the study groups gave high marks for attempting to target them and be true to them with programming. They realized FOX was willing to forego the older audience to please them, and therefore, they are very forgiving if something fails. They are just happy that someone is trying." Fessel continued, "We have been able to carve out a distinct image with our viewers. When they describe our network, they use words different from the ones they use to talk about the other networks. I heard them say we exhibited 'daring willingness to try something unique and unusual and were willing to take a chance.' We've been thanked for having programs that approach issues and current events in an entertaining format, such as our big hit, *The Simpsons*. Certainly the news-hungry and educated boomers are enjoying our program mix".

FOX wants to be a lot of things to a lot of people within the target household. Because of the variety offered, they are being seen and are maximizing their positions in those households. Since they're relative newcomers, they are still in the learning process. Most of FOX Network staff are not boomers, but the younger management staff didn't miss the cut by much and they are "young enough to learn!", said Fessel. I thank FOX for all the data and studies. But before they are analyzed, I can tell you right now that boomers are not going to change their media habits as they grow older. The idea that they'll change as they age is something that has been pounded into your head by psychologists, sociologists, and other researchers. They've drilled that fallacy into their own skulls, and have tried to do the same to you. To the extent it's believed, it can explain why a lot of businesses are losing market share and why television viewing has slipped so significantly among boomers.

Surveys should be done more often by radio stations as well as TV so they know facts about who they reach. Once a client knows you reach echo boomers and their parents, you'll have an easier sell. Additionally, I suggest stations should set up client workshops to explore and explain marketing and advertising techniques, especially to ad agencies to help them sell their clients.

I could write this a zillion times in this book. Forget about what boomers are supposed to do, and forget about the forecasts that they'll become just like their parents. Concentrate on the now, and the future will take care of itself.

But boomers will never lose their dependency on radio—

now or in their middle or senior years. At no time in the history of our country has radio had a better opportunity to capitalize on the boomers and their children than it has now. It's a dynamite chance to sell more advertising and to think about the advertising they are going to sell in the future. But remember, while it's prudent to plan *tentatively* for the future, take it one year at a time with this group. This boomer generation is too individualistic to be mass-marketed successfully.

As an important note, in the 1988 Roper survey of the children aged 7 to 17 years old who participated in family decision making, 74% of them helped decide about leisure activities, 52% of them chose where to vacation and 79% of them helped select the television programs the family watched. What's even more important, these children came from affluent and well-educated families, and that means, those who have the means to buy your products and services. Never have children had more powerful and dramatic an influence on household decisions than in this decade.

This concept of children as a power in the home is, of course, only one contributing factor to the importance of radio. I challenge anyone to name a medium that delivers more bang for the boomer buck than radio. It can target the boomer generation and their children better than any other medium, and I can prove that with the results I've gotten comparing sales and not just responses, from print, television, and the big winner—you guessed it—radio.

Bear in mind that I am not saying it is radio alone that needs to be taken into consideration. I don't want to give that impression. Even though I am a strong supporter of radio because I have seen it work for my clients more successfully than any other medium, that doesn't mean it should be the only medium employed in your campaigns. Radio, supported by a well-thought out combination of newspaper, magazine and television ads, is the best and most successful approach. Plus, the way advertisers and marketers present themselves on radio today can lend itself not only to now, but to future uses of these methods in newspapers, magazines, television, direct mail and on specialty items as well.

You'll find that boomers aren't going to be complaining about being left out of commercials the way their elders have in the past. Boomers aren't going to be that sensitive because they have done so much more. Boomers don't really feel they have missed as much as their parents, and that's obvious from the way they travel now, and aren't waiting for the "gold watch and handshake" day when they retire. They don't have to see themselves portrayed on television or in print ads to know they are important.

Boomers have impacted the media and vice-versa more than is the case for any other generation in our history. Watch for this situation to continue with boomers' children. The crossover is astounding. Boomer parents and boomer children listen to almost the same music and enjoy a number of programs together.

In the past, advertisers aimed their messages at specific segments of the population—zoomed in to specific groups. But never has the group been larger or more varied that the boomer. Demographics aimed at the 25-to-49-year-old members of the population used to reach only that age group. Now, we have echo boomers and even their grandparents as kind of a bonus audience that is often not taken into consideration. This extraordinary crossover is something that can be utilized to advertisers' best advantage.

Boomers don't have or take the time to sit glued in front of the tube, although they do have a very few favorite programs they fit into their hectic schedules and lifestyles. But almost all boomers have radios going in their cars in their "driving to success drive time." A significant number switch on the radio as soon as they get up in the morning, listen at the office and tune in as soon as they arrive home—often late—from pursuing the boomer version of the American dream.

- Radio is a *now* medium. Boomers are *now* consumers.
- Radio ads can be changed quickly. Boomers like change and variety.
- Radio costs less and appeals more to boomers than any other medium. And because the costs are comparatively low, you can use it more often to get your targeted messages to a selected audience better and faster.
- Radio uses boomers' music to best advantage, and that combination of programs featuring *their* music with ads for products and services that appeal to *their* way of living is an unbeatable combination. (But heaven help the advertiser who turns *their* sounds into elevator music or Muzak—that's an even bigger turn-off than annoying and interruptive telephone solicitation calls are for this group of consumers.)
- Radio is ideal for the active boomer man or woman. What those boomers want is information, but not too much information. They prefer their news quick and concise—they don't want to take time away from making a buck or enjoying leisure time to study issues in too much depth. This belief isn't mine alone.

Boomers put such a high value on their time that a 1989 ERA National Real Estate Poll revealed they would prefer to hire a professional to do certain jobs around the house than to do the repairs and maintenance themselves. They are more likely to want a new house than an older, restored one. For the majority, adding on to an existing home is a whale of a time commitment. Boomers would rather move, and generally into a different neighborhood, to find the home they want.

Marketing News presented some of the results of study done by the *Times Mirror Center* for the People and the Press last year. "Young people have shown much less interest in most news...[and] people now in their 30s and 40s are better informed than the under-30s group." The article continued by pointing out that all boomers were showing a "similar lack of appetite for hard news." I am not surprised the article also zeroed in on the fact that "News with a lighter touch—news programs that blend news with entertainment—are produced in response to younger people's lower levels of interest in traditional news subjects."

Radio calls for action response. Boomers like to see themselves as always doing something. Radio helps them get that feeling of motion. Remember, it's all impulse with this generation. Even if boomers hear your message and don't write down a phone number you've had repeated at least twice in your radio ad, they'll take the time to look you up if your product or service sounds exciting and makes the boomer listener jazzed about doing something to get in on the action.

When you consider that radio is *the* medium best used to create word pictures to give the listener a chance to participate, even fantasize, about the product or service, it's a constant source of wonder to me that it isn't always the first choice.

Radio offers freedom. One can listen and still be occupied doing something else, not captive of a print or television image that has to be read or watched. There perhaps are even some radio execs who don't understand the power they can offer to advertisers. Part of your job, then, might be to get them to take better advantage of their own medium to offer creative and innovative solutions to sales and marketing problems / opportunities.

One radio executive who doesn't need any additional education to convince him of the power of radio is Dan Carelli, President and General Manager of KYXY San Diego. He was formerly with KCBQ AM / FM San Diego. Both are leading boomer stations with slightly different formats. As he stated to me in the April '91 issue of *The Boomer Report*, "Our station's steady clients keep coming back because of the powerful sales results they get. But potential advertisers who aren't on our station take a 'wait and see' attitude. Their lack of education on the boomers makes them hold back. Remember, not everyone understands the purchasing power of radio. And it's not pitched by the advertising agencies— because we don't have the big dollars in production that TV does. Radio is a little more complicated to buy—but the rewards can be enormous." Would it surprise you to hear me second that motion resoundingly?

For radio to be fully effective, you have to run at least fifteen 60-second commercials each day, between 5 a.m. and 8 p.m. in equal rotation. Also, you should use at least four to five stations over a two-to four-week period to guarantee market penetration. And don't ignore stations that are nine, ten and eleven down the list. Boomers have a lot of similarities, but they also have a lot of differences. You don't want to lose any potential customers by leaving stations out of your broadcasting loop.

A benefit to using radio that shouldn't be overlooked is the promotional aspect. Radio stations are naturals for this win-win arrangement. To boost their listening audience, many stations hold contests. Why not have your product or service mentioned time and time again as the prize? In a tight economy, that's a great way to generate more response.

If you've been "married" to newspaper and magazine ads because you think you need actual print, or glossy four-color ads, you're not only making an error to ignore radio, you are making a crucial mistake. Boomers listen to radio more than they watch television. They listen to radio more than they read magazines of all types and newspapers. I'm not talking about acid rock stations. I'm referring to adult contemporary, country and western, jazz, talk and news formats. Modern country, in particular, holds a strong boomer audience because they have updated in the last twenty years. The success rate from this entire mix is especially prevalent in West Coast markets, but holds true all across the country.

The hottest radio format is the oldies-of-all-time phenomenon which last year was up more than 166% since 1985. The sheer number of boomers supports this growth, and the 25 to 54-year-old group with discretionary income is the bunch that advertisers are after. Only the very oldest end of this scale falls out of boomer range. But because of the boomers, with influence reaching both forward and back, what appeals to them also appeals to those in much younger and much older age groups.

Boomers and their children are the most potent audience marketers and advertisers have. When you look at the Arbitron ratings for a radio station that shows a #1 rating for a very young listening audience, say 12 to 24 years of age, you're also going to find that same station rated among the top ten for listeners age 25 to 49. Boomers listen to their children's music. This means the boomers and their kids share tastes. It's very different from what was the case when the boomers grew up and had parents who couldn't stand the kids' music and wouldn't even listen to it.

This unique tie-in of the current shared musical tastes and listening habits between boomers and their offspring should be the foundation of the marketing thrust that should be used to appeal to this huge listening audience. Of course, you'll have to have good creative production to go along with any advertising. What your ad sounds like makes all the difference in the world.

Another tip to help you market and sell is a hint about the female boomer. Radio is particularly effective in reaching working women. Research shows that up to 70% of them are tuned in sometime during the working day. If you run an ad, whether print, television, or radio, design it to appeal to both men and women, and that applies if you run an advertisement in a sports section or a men's magazine or in a women's magazine or women's section of a newspaper.

Now I'm not saying to ignore print, television and direct mail. What I am saying, even *urging,* is that you use radio as the keystone around which you build your full media approach.

How can marketers best use radio?

• *Psychographics are more important than demographics.* As I've said, the boomer mind-set affects consumers ten years older and younger than the boomers themselves. The news, talk and sports stations may skew older than the boomers, but it's the over-35 boomers who have more discretionary income; boomers affect every radio format in the country. And boomers' children—who heavily influence family buying decisions—are tuning in to the lite-FM stations whose music relies on the golden oldies. When you sell to the 77 million boomers on radio, you get their 42 million children as a bonus.

• *Don't believe that the boomer is too broke to spend money.* Eighty percent of them own credit cards and over a third charged $1,000 or more last year. Boomers are increasingly moving into higher salary brackets. And, as many of them are entrepreneurs, the sky's the limit for a significant number of them. I'm surely not ignoring the fact that many working boomers are not in the earnings stratosphere, but even the blue collar crowd feels some entitlement to the good things in life, even if they have to come on a more modest scale. Catch this new wrinkle. Boomers are signing on the dotted line so echo boomers can learn the joys of charging with their own (with a credit limit) versions of Mastercard. Like father, like son, was never truer!

- *Don't project too far ahead.*

No matter what a boomer's age or income, don't project too far or you'll get blind sided. Psychologists and futurists can't foresee what boomers will like or dislike through their life cycles. With this generation, you must take one year at a time. You have to stay light on your feet with these consumers. If you try to predict the future, you won't sell your products and services now.

- *Don't rush the "modern maturity" approach.*

There are still 20 million boomers in their twenties; until 1995, there will be 40 million in their thirties. It won't be until 2010 that the bulk of boomers will turn fifty. Stop worrying about their middle-age profile and what they'll be like as seniors— boomers don't want to talk about it, so why should you? Don't rush this "mature marketing" approach in your copy. Besides the fact that there are still 20 million boomers in their twenties, even when the boomers are "seniors" they'll never think like seniors. I think Adrian Callus, vice-president of media for Gray Advertising in New York, said it best: "You just don't turn 50 and throw away *Time* magazine to start reading *Modern Maturity.*" To paraphrase Ms. Callus, I say today's radio listeners don't tune out their favorite radio stations to listen to learned discourses or staid music when they attain a certain age, either.

To reinforce the point above, CBS television finally realized it had to get the boomer market. Why else would it revamp its programming to appeal to boomer viewers and their children? If the aging population were truly the hot market, do you really think CBS would have made so drastic a switch?

- *Media buyers vastly underuse radio.*

Radio accounts for less than 7% of total advertising dollars spent. Media planners should use radio for aggressive niche marketing, for which it's the natural medium: radio is local by nature, and that's what every marketer is looking for, a way to target a specific consumer. Radio buys can produce results. The hotel industry, for example, sells more room packages on radio than any other medium. For many reasons, radio is the best long-term buy around. And throughout this chapter, and, in fact, throughout this book, I'll give marketers and advertisers the reasons and the incentives they need to double the paltry 7% they've been spending each year on national radio buys.

- *Use the KISS theory - "Keep It Simple, Stupid!"*

Don't try to get too sophisticated with your marketing approach to the boomers. Make your pitch to the point, intelligently, and with some excitement. Don't get too gimmicky.

The United States will continue to be a youth-focused culture. A new baby boom is underway. As of the end of 1989, the birth rate exceeded four million (underestimated by the Census bureau, but predicted by *The Boomer Report* a year earlier) which is where we were when the baby boom ended on December 31, 1964. Our country will always be youth oriented at any age. Do you see the Rolling Stones retiring? Is Cher wearing any more clothes than she used to? Rock 'n' Roll will live forever.

To help prove my observations about radio, read on and learn what Robert K. Moore, Executive Vice-President of Westwood One Stations Group, Incorporated, has to say in "The Great Communicator: What Effect Does Radio Have on the Baby Boomer Generation?" He has noted: "Baby boomers were raised on radio, from portable radios to clock radios to carry-along boom boxes to Sony Walkmans to car radios. The boomers are definitely the radio generation. If you were born between 1938 and 1958, then you were very much a part of the radio revolution. In the early '60s rock 'n' roll and MOR (Middle of the Road—Nat King Cole, Bobby Darin, Elvis Presley, The Mills Brothers, etc.) dominated the AM dial. Then in the middle '60s the British Invasion hit—The Beatles, The Rolling Stones, Jerry and the Pacemakers, Herman's Hermits—and radio exploded once again.

"But during this time something very peculiar happened; a strange and formidable relationship started to develop. Radio started to move from one side of the dial to the next. It moved from the safe harbor of AM to the dark, secretive, and interference-free FM side of the radio dial. In the mid-and-late '60s, FM radio really blossomed and this furthered the boomers' incredible, insatiable taste for music that was broadcast static-free, with fewer commercials, less hype, and better stereo separation. FM radio was born and it blossomed very quickly. As the boomers' lifestyles changed, the usage of radio increased.

"Throughout the '70s, as radios became more transportable, boomers became more and more attached to them. Soon there would be Walkmans, radios you could put at your side and take with you anywhere. The clock radio had moved from the bedroom, to the bathroom, to the kitchen. The car radio became a means for communication on transit to and from work. You can't go into a major city or transportation center without seeing earphones on the heads of hundreds of people. Radio has been and always will be 'the take-along' medium.

"Radio today enjoys its greatest diversity and also allows for the greatest precision for target marketing. In the '50s and '60s, advertisers tried to reach the lucrative 18 to 54-year-old audience, and tried to incorporate the teenager, the mother and the father in one message. In the late '70s and '80s, target marketing became a niche word and people started to recognize certain age groups had similar patterns. They learned that baby boomers who were born in the rock 'n' roll era were not going to change their music listening habits or usage of other media just because they turned 30 or 35 or 40 or 45 or even 50 years old. These researchers found that baby boomers had something very much in common. They responded greatly to radio, they believed in radio, they trusted radio, they grew up with radio and they developed passionate loyalties to radio personalities and radio stations. They followed the development, the growth and even the death of certain favorite stations, for example, KMET and KHJ Boss Radio, both in Los Angeles. These people became affected by the media, they learned terminology and buzz words. They were exposed to the evolution and change of the music industry. They watched Bruce Springsteen develop on the radio into America's folk hero. They listened and watched Bob Dylan spend twenty-five years developing his own story through the radio. They followed stations that started in the '60s doing nothing but news and developed into international news services. They listened and became intertwined with the development of talk radio and talk show hosts. Baby boomers devote a large portion of their time to radio. It's their friend from childhood with their six-dollar Japanese portable radio to their new BMW with a sixteen pre-set top of the line Alpine stereo. Radio continues to be the dominant medium for the boomers.

"Radio has the unique ability to target the 18 to 24-year-old, the 25 to 54-year-old , the 35 to 44-year-old and the 45 to 54-year-old audiences. By segregating the audiences, varying formats, and by using combination spectrum buys, you'll be able to reach a niche target. Radio is by far the most cost-efficient medium and is the medium of immediacy. Within forty-eight hours any advertiser can be on any radio station in the United States. No other medium offers that kind of turn-around, and for production values, nothing beats a dramatic radio commercial. I'm sure everybody has a favorite radio commercial that could be played back in his or her mind right now.

"Radio is an inexpensive medium that gets tremendous response, has incredible reach and offers an unlimited frequency. Something niche marketers discovered many years ago is that radio is the medium to use to reach the boomers. If profit is your motive, then effectively communicating to your target audience has to be your goal, and radio reigns number one. The beauty of radio is that it's been "pronounced dead" three times. It's still very much alive. In the early '50s, television "killed" radio, yet it continued to grow. In the '70s, it was all the new technologies, tape players, cassettes—does anybody remember eight-track tapes? They were all going to replace the radio. In the '80s, it was again all the new technologies, compact disc players, direct audio broadcasts, cable television, cable radio. Yet through it all, radio has continued to nurture, gain strength and retain that incredible loyalty from its true believers, the boomers.

"If you were born between 1937 and 1968, years that encompass the entire baby boom and then some, you know what your favorite medium is, you know where you go, when you want to hear the news, when you want to know what's happening in music, when you want to listen to your favorite talk show personality, or when you just want to enjoy your favorite sport, news, weather, music, or information. All of that is provided to you in massive quantities by your best friend, the radio."

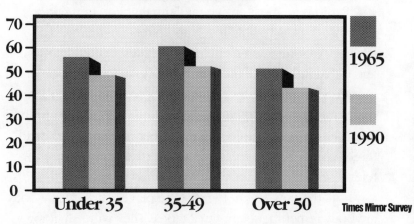

Media and the Boomer • *Radio*

1965

1990

Times Mirror Survey

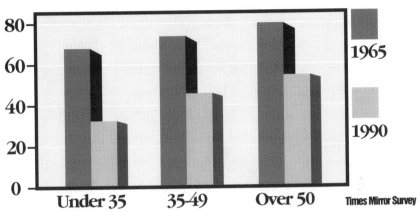

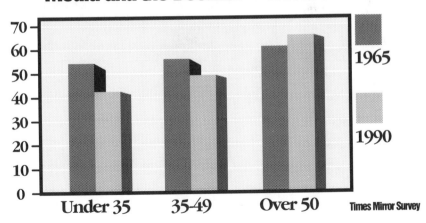

CHAPTER 4

Hotel and Travel

Boomers take their vacations - NOW!

In a hurried world of lasers, FAX, instant food and other rapid miracles of the twentieth century, it's no surprise that travel has become rushed as well. Yes, the boomer mentality has significantly revolutionized the entire industry of leisure and business travel. As a matter of record, 85% of all travel planners who affect the travel industry are boomers.

Based on a 1988 survey of 1500 hotel and motel guests by CONSTAT National Lodging Consumer Data Base of San Francisco, which features statistics exclusively for the travel industry, "Fifty-three percent of all hotel / motel guests nationwide are boomers. They pay more than the national average for room rates, participate in more frequent-stay

programs, take more business trips and travel more for
pleasure and personal reasons. Their average length of stay is
longer and they are usually planning more business trips
within a 12-month period. Further, the mean household
income of the national average of all hotel guests surveyed is
$46,000. The boomer's average is $53,000. Incidentally, the
female corporate traveler represents 59% of personal and
pleasure travelers and 65% of all conventioneers." (She will be
discussed in a later chapter on the woman boomer.)
Obviously, boomers are changing the way the hotel and travel
industries will sell themselves over the next 30 years of
boomer adulthood.

An important fact to remember is that the same mind-set
of the boomers for business travel isn't far from their attitude
toward leisure travel. They do it quickly, impulsively and they
do it to make themselves and their companies look good.
Most of the more affluent boomers are in hard hitting careers,
success-oriented and not a little nervous about their status.
They react to hotels in the same way they do to other
products and services. They do, however, consider leisure
travel their number one stress reliever.

Los Angeles Times reporter Edwin Chen wrote in
August of 1991, "Vacations will change: The travel industry,
for instance, will see more and more people taking short
vacations because it is increasingly difficult for two-job
families to coordinate long ones." Chen added, "There will
also be a resurgence of winter vacations as the children of
two-career couples grow up and leave home, forecasters say."

If hotel owners have even a glimmering of understanding
of what motivates their customers, why then is there an
oversupply of hotel rooms in this country? Of course, there
are plenty of reasons we won't get into at this time. But one
of the reasons hoteliers are having a problem is that they have

not properly identified their target market for advertising. Some of them continue to define their audience as the "over-50" maturing customer with discretionary income for their leisure travel. That attitude won't work today. The primary focus of the hotelier should be the boomer. He or she has the best customer profile for many reasons, one of which is the crossover factor. If they are at a hotel for leisure, they might, if they are encouraged by the facility, inspect the property for a future meeting.

The following letter, from the director of marketing at The Westin La Paloma in Tuscon, gives a perfect example of what I am saying here:

Dear Phil:

What a summer! While the final numbers have not been counted, conservative projections are 20% over plan. And if you take into account our unadvertised golf package sales, undoubtedly influenced by our radio ads, that statistic jumps to 40%.

Almost exclusively, Phil, it was radio that put the magic in our Summer Magic Getaway package. Prior to the radio campaign we did direct mail to previous guests. But the response to this medium is not reflected in the above projections. Midway through the campaign we placed our message on 32 movie screens in Phoenix and Tucson. And finally, display ads ran in the June and July America West in-flight magazines. Most frequently, however, radio was mentioned by our guests as the medium that influenced their decisions. Put it all together and the result is more than 16,000 room nights, establishing 1991 as the best summer for leisure travel in the six year history of The Westin La Paloma.

Why so successful? The right product at the right price. Knowing our audience (the boomer). The right message on the right medium. And, of course, the reach and frequency of our campaign that you so expertly negotiated with radio stations in Phoenix and Tucson!

Looking back, the marketing strategy never concerned me. But negotiating was a risk, relatively new to us as a tool, at least in such a large amount. Happily, and probably not surprisingly, the program is working well. This can be attributed to your careful execution of procedures and the on-site training for staff throughout the resort that preceded the campaign. Plus your constant follow-up allowed us to keep things on track. Perhaps the ongoing confidence and support of our controller gives final validation to your professionalism and commitment.

Many thanks, Phil, for your contribution to the success of The Westin La Paloma this summer. Very soon, we should begin to discuss next year.

Enthusiastically,

Ed Schwitzky
Director of Marketing

What follows is an expansion of Ed Schwitzky's very kind letter to me. They are both included to validate and to reinforce some of the things I've written in this book, and while I admit I enjoy the ego stroking, that's not the only reason his observations are reprinted. Examples of what works, how it works, and why it works are a lot more important than having somebody mount a soap box with a "because I said so, that's why," attitude.

"True to Phil's projections, leisure travel to The Westin La Paloma this year has been strongly regional. And, not surprisingly, if you trust Phil, many travelers are getting away for short periods, seemingly to escape the pressures and tensions of day-to-day life. Our audience is the boomer - median age 44 years, manager or executive, with a household income of more than $100,000.

"In view of the lingering recession, it was expected that travel decisions would become more price-driven. Instead, consumers placed an even greater emphasis on value. Making sure they got their money's worth, and a little bit more. Taking great care of oneself and family was the unspoken mission.

"Response to our organized children's program has been interesting. Parents desire to reunite the family for a few days of fun, rather than segregate adults and kids. Consequently, the most popular programs are half-day activities and evening movies, allowing mom and dad brief respites of togetherness.

"Traditionally, summer trade at The Westin La Paloma is largely intra-state travel. While the summer of 1991 was no different, it was the most successful summer for leisure travel in the resort's six-year history.

"Why? Listening and responding to the needs, wants and expectations of our market (the boomer). Midway through last summer, prospective guests expressed resistance to our promotion that provided a credit for food, beverage and resort recreation. Their interest was to pay only 'the price of admission' that is the cost of the room. Additional purchases, they decided, should be discretionary. The price-driven orientation, at least for the summer, continued into this year. And we responded with bare-bones, value-added room pricing.

"Besides price and knowing our market, product had a lot to do with our success. Plus, the right message and the right medium. And very importantly the reach and frequency of our campaign that Phil so expertly crafted with radio stations in Tucson and Phoenix.

"Clearly, radio is an effective medium with boomers. Almost exclusively, it was radio that put the "magic" in our Summer Magic Getaway package. The campaign was supported by direct mail to previous guests, movie-screen messages and display ads in one in-flight magazine. But most frequently, radio was mentioned by our guests as the medium that influenced their decisions. If you take into account our unadvertised golf package sales, undoubtedly influenced by our radio spots, the results for this summer exceed our historical average by nearly 60%.

"The Westin La Paloma is a 487-room deluxe destination resort in Tucson, Arizona. It boasts 27 holes of golf on a Jack Nicklaus-designed course, a dozen tennis courts (including four clay courts), a health club, five restaurants and three lounges, and a free-form pool featuring a water slide and swim-up bar."

Ed Schwitzky has been the marketing director for The Westin La Paloma for two years. Previously, Ed spent eleven years in the greater Phoenix area, including eight years in various sales and marketing positions at the Arizona Biltmore. It is important to understand how this attitude of blending business and pleasure occurred. The boomer is the best-educated, most-traveled group in the history of this country. They are the generation reared in the glow of parental prosperity. However, boomers became rebellious toward the material concerns they had taken for granted. But by the time members of this group reached their mid-twenties, the economy was eroding along with their illusions. They were now destined to become forever preoccupied with money— getting it and spending it. Disappointed and disillusioned by the realities of a bleak economy and often frozen in a dreary job market, the Now generation is stressed and clamoring for escape. But like everything else in their lives, nothing is to be wasted, especially their precious time. They, therefore, devised a way to combine business and leisure by tagging on a few days after a business meeting or arranging a client visit to coincide with a scheduled vacation.

In order to evaluate and capitalize on this important psychology of the traveling population, it is important to understand the economic forces behind their attitude toward business and pleasure travel. The boomers were the group most affected by the perils of industry in the '70s and '80s. They were first-hand witnesses to double-digit unemployment, wage freezes, and the downward spiral of their savings account interest. The Official Yuppie Handbook now but a wasteful dream, they became obsessed with their struggle to stay afloat. Paying their bills, planning for their children's college and grandma's rest home became the order of the day.

This shift toward economic survival is one of the strongest factors reshaping the attitude of the tourism industry. The standard two-week vacation in mid-summer with the whole family tumbling out of the station wagon onto the sand has been replaced by quick jaunts any weekend — anywhere there's a special rate offer. The hotel guest of today and for the next three decades will be looking for special packages at reasonable rates from properties that offer the most amenities and that are willing to spoil them and make them feel good. To continue the "spoiling" that many over-indulged boomers have received since they were in their cradles won't hurt the industry. Who doesn't like to feel pampered and singled out for "special" attention?

Don't forget, though, with boomers, mentioning that you are offering something for a limited time has a lot of appeal to their inclinations to act on impulse.

The boomer looks at hotels also for value and safety. Since boomers travel with their children to hotel destinations more than any other generation in history, it is wise to anticipate their presence. They do not want to be away from their children any more than they have to and they even feel guilty if they spend too much time at work during those trips. Hoteliers are greatly affected by this situation. This is a market positioning issue for the hotel industry.

As an example, the Lake Arrowhead Hilton in Southern

California did exceptionally well with the boomer. Boomers were responding to ads with special package prices, and because of those prices, they brought their children with them. Boomers don't want to leave their children in a room with a baby sitter. Hotels that respond by having planned activities for the children are the hotels boomers will patronize. The small cost of providing those activities pays for itself in a flash and leads to repeat business, a must for any property, but even more crucial for resorts. When I started working with this property almost five years ago, the occupancy rate was dismal. We worked together to create a special package that included ski lift tickets.

To quote my 1990 *San Diego Business Journal* interview concerning the Lake Arrowhead Hilton: "The minute the ads hit the radio, the hotel started getting 300 calls a day, with about 135 reservations daily. I thought I'd died and gone to heaven. Within two and a half weeks, they'd booked reservations through Easter." I learned a lot during that campaign, but was most struck by the fact more than 80% of the telephone calls came from women boomers. That kind of learning experience has been priceless for my clients and me. Neither they nor I will ever make the error of discounting the woman traveler!

Last summer, I worked with the Sheraton Park Central Towers in Dallas. The problem? The usual. Too many empty rooms. Again, radio helped solve the problem in a big, fast way! We helped them do 8000 room nights! It's no mystery to me that hotels have to market a lot harder at present than they used to. Overbuilding has caused part of the dilemma; stiff competition for too few recession dollars is the other side of the coin.

Boomers' children are the next generation coming up to whom hoteliers will have to pay close attention, even though they are a smaller group. Hoteliers will have to cater to these children because, by traveling with their parents, they have been exposed more to the hotel industry than were the boomers. This view is supported by Dorothy Jordon, editor of *Travel with Your Children,* a New York-based monthly newsletter that tracks the family travel market.

She has written,"The baby boom generation is the best-traveled generation ever, and as parents, they want to vacation with their kids while still having time to pursue adult activities. And they are looking for places where the family is welcome, not just tolerated."

The hotel industry and its relationship to the boomer children was considerably influenced by the emergence of the female boomer. In compliance with her attitude of merging career and motherhood, thereby "having it all," she caused children's activities to become more closely aligned with their parents' activities. For many years, the hotel industry's posture on hotel travel which included most of the airlines as well as car rental agencies, was that the upper income amenities belonged strictly to the 50+ group and for the real money, that was the target group. That attitude worked until the early 1980s.

Women at that time represented less than 25% of the higher end work force. Last year, the female boomer did at least 40% or more of all business travel. The American Hotel and Motel Association noted this year that female business travel is increasing three times as fast as travel by their male counterparts. With the dual-paycheck family income, they have the money and clout to do it. However, along with two people working in the same family and all the ensuing sociological changes, there is also the major effect on family life styles. For example, the cruise lines have had only seven, ten and fourteen-day cruises. Now one sees cruise lines advertising an abundance of three and four-day cruises on television, radio and in newspapers. What do you think that's all about? That's about discretionary income, the need to escape for a quick getaway and certainly not geared to the 50+ traveler who can plan well ahead. Some hotels, however, have now made significant changes in the type of accommodations and amenities offered. Those on the marketing ball now offer the best rooms, the best food, and the best service to their best customers—the boomers. It appears today that senior citizens and foreign travelers are willing to do without some of the plush extras during their vacations. Boomers expect more—that's part of their mind-set—and now they are getting more.

My intention is to present and solve the problem of addressing the wrong issues when marketing the hotels. The psychologists who have been speaking and writing on the subject have been blind sided by facts drawn from the AARP—the American Association of Retired Persons. The research firms are quoting the wrong figures to the travel industry, thereby wreaking havoc on the hotels. Any information the experts provide that deals with matters prior to 1987 is obsolete with regard to marketing the hotel industry to the boomer.

There are reasons to make a marketing shift. As we know, boomers are impulsive, compulsive spenders. They have not put enough money away to vacation and travel extensively when they retire as had been done by some former, more traditional persons. Rather, they will continue to resent their parents' philosophy of saving for a vacation—someday. To repeat, boomers will be teenagers until the day they die. As the boomers influence persons both younger and older than themselves, even seniors are not acting as seniors used to. From the hotel industry standpoint, the seniors are an important element of their business, but nowadays they must be approached in the same manner as the boomer because so many seniors have a younger mind-set than their ages might indicate. Boomers won't act as traditional seniors have. Instead, it's more likely that a growing number of seniors will have to be marketed in the same way boomers are, by an appeal to youthfulness. As a group, boomers will not be successfully marketed as seniors; fewer of them than one might expect will seek senior discounts. The appeal to boomers lies in quality "specials." Romantic getaway packages will continue to appeal to them far into their senior years. Although seniors have an important role in today's marketplace, they will not exist as the same group for the next thirty years.

One of the reasons hoteliers are having difficulty filling their properties is that they are using shotgun approaches based on outdated demographics. Today's customer is highly susceptible to impulse buying of perceived value. You provide the impetus, and just watch the boomer provide the buying power! I would be remiss if I didn't point out one major consideration for the entire hotel industry. It may be part, and a crucially important part, of the entire travel and tourism industry, but each hotel is in a particular market and location, and therefore calls for individual marketing and advertising. Ms. Stein may have written "a rose is a rose is a rose," but each and every hotel has significant differences that can be exploited, even if "a hotel is a hotel is a hotel."

A second serious consideration is the fact that far too many hoteliers rely strictly on their ad agencies to get the job done for them. Unless an ad agency has worked *successfully* with hotels, the hotelier should direct the advertising and marketing campaigns. And even if you are dealing with a "winner" agency, your hand on the tiller helps assure your efforts move in the proper direction. Because most hotel management lacks advertising expertise, there is too little guidance given to agencies handling (or mishandling) their accounts. Hoteliers should consider enrolling key management in junior college or night school advertising courses so that they better understand how to communicate with the media and advertising agencies. Once this knowledge is gained, hoteliers will be less likely to succumb to fancy commercials and "image" advertising they can watch or read because they'll have so few persons occupying the rooms! I think they'd be happier being too busy dealing with zillions of boomer reservations instead.

When I did a survey of various hotel schools in this country I learned that in their three and four-year programs in hotel management, only a few offered ten to fifteen weeks of three-hour classes in advertising—as an elective. Hotel schools should put greater emphasis on teaching advertising so that future hoteliers are better prepared than their predecessors. The hotel industry lags fifteen years behind in advertising and marketing education. It needs to play catch-up immediately. It has to learn that "location, location, location," listed as the three main reasons a vacation site is chosen, doesn't wash today. If you make your property sound unique, within reason, boomers won't much care where you are. And don't be afraid of hurting your corporate image by giving special rates. The few dollars you may not see on one end of the room price will be returned to you many fold by repeat business at regular rates. You're in an entirely different ball game selling rooms as part of the complete travel package. Only a hotelier will understand what that means and take advantage of it. *Image* advertising will do very little to help your property in the '90s. Instead, you'll need to put more *hard sell* into your advertising and marketing campaigns.

Here's an example of what we did to measure the results of our advertising campaign for a small inn nestled in California's Santa Cruz Mountains. This three-star property with all the amenities for romantic weekends and for think tank get-togethers is near the Silicon Valley. That makes it perfect for executives in the electronics industry to use the site for group meetings and a little R&R.

For a two-week period each, we advertised special packages in the newspaper; then we ran the offer on radio; and finally, we ran television spots on news and prime time programs. We observed the following results.

From radio, the property received an average of fourteen calls a day and booked 35% of the callers during that contact. Seven calls daily resulted from the newspaper ad, and 50% of those callers booked. Fewer than 5% of the twenty-five to thirty persons who called because they saw the ad on television booked into the property.

The reason the Inn at Saratoga booked more rooms from the radio commercials is because radio can target the boomer better than any other medium used by the hotel industry to sell rooms for both leisure and business. The results from this example are typical of my experience with other properties in the country during the last five years. It shows the positive effects of advertising in the markets accessible by car, something that must be done unless a property is near an airport and convenient to reach from any point on the globe. Even then, it doesn't hurt to donate a few marketing bucks to the auto-accessible markets. But keep in mind that more than 85% of all domestic vacation travel is by automobile, truck, or recreational vehicle, as reported by the American Automobile Association.

These findings are borne out by a study done in California

by the Long Beach Area Convention and Visitors Council. Personal or rental cars were the predominant method of transportation used by visitors to attractions in that area.

Results such as those just mentioned above were repeated in many other cases. A short radio campaign on boomer stations in San Francisco for the Carmel Valley Ranch in California netted bookings for 200 room nights, and those were boomer bookings at a property that normally catered to the older, upscale market. Ditto for the spots in Los Angeles offering special weekends for couples. Boomer stations, again, netted the Portofino Inn a booking windfall. From the 358 calls received by the staff, 258 room nights went into the booking ledger.

If you own a resort property, as I'll show over and over with hotel success story examples, radio can be extremely effective because it's inexpensive to produce audio and air commercial spots. Their range is broad, and you are free to alter them quickly to reflect changes in your marketing plan.

Here are a few other aspects of hotel marketing to consider. If you have in-house, closed circuit television, describe both your property and the interesting things to see and do in the surrounding area. The appeal of this isn't limited to the boomer, but boomers especially like information in such a handy form and format. Develop informational tent cards for each room, and have similar collateral material at the front desk. When you have guests at your property for business, encourage them to return for vacations when leisure tops the chart. If guests are there for leisure, offer them some incentives as "special" guests so they'll consider returning (and you hope, with a large gang from their firm) for business purposes—at great rates. Offer to show them around the entire property. Let the boomer carry your advertising for you. You know what they say about word of mouth.

Would you like to increase the response rate to your questionnaires? When you ask a customer to fill one out, give that customer something, like a free continental breakfast. As the national average for the return of marketing questionnaires is a gloomy 3%, increasing that tenfold by giving a couple of croissants and a cup of coffee to a respondent is indeed a savvy investment.

Publicize your property to prior guests by sending out a flier or brochure plus a personal letter every three or four months to tell them about activities and attractions at or near your hotel. Offer special discounts from time to time during the year.

Travel agents can become part of your army of salespeople. Travel agents are devoting more and more of their energies in an attempt to garner more of the corporate travel business. One way to get these agents to sell more rooms for you is to mention them in your radio commercials with a 10-second tag on the ads you run in their market area. This program has proven very successful.

By no stretch of the imagination am I counseling you to ignore the senior market. Just go after it differently. For them, ads through direct mail, newspapers and their special interest magazines reap big benefits. If you advertise special rates for seniors, and hold senior functions, you'll get and keep seniors' business. Try to keep in mind that the seniors have a strong tendency to keep their bucks in the sugar bowl or in the bank. Keep prices a bit on the low side and you'll see repeat bookings you otherwise might miss. No matter the amount of wealth seniors might have or hoard, they have a psychology different from the boomers and their proclivity towards impulse spending.

Lately, there's been a significant increase in the effort to market an entire state as a vacation destination. Active travel, tourism and lodging associations are loudly beating the drums to attract visitors to their geographical area. Various locales and destinations have targeted themselves to *select* groups of people, rather than splashing logos and catchy slogans across the newspaper travel sections, although there's a great deal of that done, too. States of the Union advertising expenditures have soared. Don't tell me you haven't seen an attractive billboard in the warm Southwest urging you to "Ski Utah."

Bill A. Crabtree, Vice President of Western Region Sales for Gannett Outdoor Network, USA, has some thought-provoking things to say about the outdoor advertising field that I will paraphrase. He tells his clients that boomer families work more hours than their parents did, and while they may have more money to spend, have less time in which to do so. He has found, and I tend to agree, that boomers spend their limited free time with their friends and families. According to Crabtree, "Boomers who do read, usually don't read the entire paper. . . boomers care less for hard news than prior generations. . . newspapers cannot achieve high frequency without multiple insertions due to their short shelf life. Most importantly," he states, "Unless boomers are looking for an ad it may be missed." They have very little time to spend reading print media advertisements, and even less for watching television. He's observed that even with efforts for higher quality television programming, "People Meters" show viewing on a downward slide, partly because of the proliferation of alternatives to television. Crabtree makes his points with more than a little style, and it's easy to agree with a discussion presented with a zippy combination of examples and knowledge grounded in his experience in the business. Without stating it explicitly, he shows the value of good, even great, copy in any medium. I know from my own experience that it's a lot harder to write a 10-second radio spot than it is for a longer format. Outdoor advertising, caught as one zooms along the road, has an even bigger challenge in the copywriting arena, and my hat is off to anyone who can do the marketing job so well in so short a span of time and such a relatively small space as a billboard or other outdoor ad. (Besides, how could I argue with a man who shares so many of my own views?)

He feels the combination of radio as an audio medium, with outdoor advertising as the visual one seen by zillions of boomers, is the way to go. That combination works superbly to keep a product or service at the top of the consumer's mind. Crabtree restates findings concerning boomers' reading habits. He supports my view, and the view of many experts, that boomers don't have the time to read. Because they have so many interests, even if they do read niche publications, not one of them is going to come even close to capturing all of them. His clinching argument concerning the value of outdoor advertising is the fact that newspapers, magazines, radio and television use that format to advertise their publications or stations!

Even if you're not an avid watcher of television, you've surely noticed the ads tempting you to visit Mexico. No matter what state you're in, you have golden chances to coattail onto your state's big push to get visitors there. But to be sure it's your hotel they choose as the place to lodge, you have the challenge to make yourself unique and more attractive than the place next door or right down the road. It's one thing to get them where they live, it's quite another to get them to live, temporarily, with you—as a guest at your facility! Offer price, amenities and quality. Get a handle on *who* actually comes to your hotel. Compare that profile to the potential guest you are trying to reach. See how reality may differ from dream projections. Then, adjust, and adjust some more.

The hotel industry is the last one into a recession and the last one out. By the year 2000, many believe tourism will be the leading industry all over the country, as it already is in California, Hawaii and Florida. Why? A main reason is, as I've previously stated, that boomers are not going to wait for years to go on vacations the way their parents did. They're not going to defer their pleasure and wait until retirement after working some thirty years to take a two or three-week vacation. Boomer vacations may be shorter—a lot shorter— and they take their leisure time in spurts, but *now* and *often.*

Take a look at what Marilyn Block, executive vice-president of the NAISBITT GROUP, a Washington, D.C., research firm specializing in forecasting trends, says. She predicts, "In the 1990s, the tradition of the two-week vacation will disappear. It will be replaced by the custom of taking weekend vacations scattered throughout the year. The major reason for this is that a large number of 'Baby Boomers' will be filling mid-level management positions, leading to fierce competition for the few upper-level jobs. They'll be unwilling to take a two-week block of time off from work. They won't want to be conspicuous by their absence. Instead, they'll take four or five weekend vacations a year..."

Doubletree Inns were planned and built to serve weekday business needs and although there was a good occupancy rate on Saturdays and Sundays as well, management wanted to increase that portion of business. I helped them to reach this goal by working with them to develop their highly successful "Weekend Warrior" campaign.

According to U.S. Data Travel of Washington, D.C., those under 35 represent 46% of all domestic trips that were taken in 1989. Of these domestic trips, 34% of the travelers were 35 to 54, with the leading edge being boomers. Only 20% were in age 55+ group. I bring this up to help change your mind-set concerning advertising approaches.

The tourism industry, hotels in particular, is going to have to change its mind-set. In the past, they have gone after what they call "discretionary income." And they've made, and continue to make a serious error by believing that boomers aren't the spenders. Marketers and advertisers in these industries have to stop thinking that the influential money lines the pockets or fills the bank accounts of only the older generation. As a telling example, when you have a boomer couple at your property for any reason, you are very likely to be dealing with *two* people who influence a much wider travel sphere. He may be on the search committee for the planned product show sometime down the road. She may be in charge of booking her company's next big convention. And

Domestic Travel

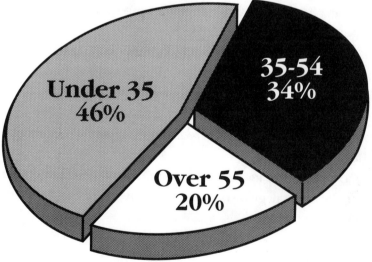

Under 35
46%

35-54
34%

Over 55
20%

they may be planning a trip with their children at some point, and could even be considering a group vacation with extended family and friends. Don't let these marketing opportunities pass you by.

True, the over-50 group controls most of the nation's wealth and 80% of its bank savings accounts. That's great for the financial institutions, but not for the hotel industry, considering that most of the business travelers and conventioneers are boomers. I've been exclusive to the tourism industry now for almost 20 years, and I've handled the plushest of the plush four-and five-star hotel properties in the United States, and I can tell you the 55+ group has done nothing for the hotel industry - -absolutely nothing.

Statistics released in Long Beach, California, in the study mentioned earlier, certainly support my contention that boomers are the ones doing the travelling and spending those all-important tourist dollars. Let me quote from that study: "In the 1990 annual period, two-thirds of all surveyed visitors to Long Beach were between the ages of 25 and 44 years. The median annual household income of surveyed visitor groups. . . was calculated to be $52,800."

Business meetings, conventions, new product shows, leisure travel, trips with children, romantic getaways, and quickie R & R trips are boomer-driven. They can be the salvation of the entire hotel industry simply by the sheer force of their numbers and the incredible power of the megabucks they have to spend.

Be aggressive in marketing and advertising to the boomers in the '90s; it will give you the competitive edge that you need to sell more rooms!

CHAPTER 5

Money

Boomers want it all - NOW!

The boomer has been blamed for the current state of the economy, when instead, the economy should be blamed for the boomer. The current recession has zilch to do with the boomer.

In 1988, there were 74 million people aged 43 to 65, and 22 million of them earned more than $40,000. Also in 1988, there were 77 million people aged 24 to 42, and almost 26 million of them earned more than $40,000. Those figures, of course, are even higher today. So when you talk about the older generation and discretionary income, just looking at the figures here shows you why boomers and their children are really your target market no matter what you're selling.

Admittedly, the way they are spending money now may mean they won't have that much to spend in later years. No one really knows for sure. Not even boomers themselves!

Let's look at what happened between 1984 and 1988. In 1984, those aged 25-44 represented 44% of those earning more than $50,000-$100,000+ annually. By 1988, the percentage of the affluent in the 25 to 44-year-old age range had risen to 47%. The percentage of the affluent in the 45 to 65-year-old range decreased to 43% in 1988, from 47% in 1984. In 1989 alone, boomers earned $985 billion. That's right, billion!

If boomers don't scrimp and scrape the way their parents did, who can blame them? If they decide to get under a designer umbrella and go out and spend, spend, spend, rather than save for a rainy day, do today's financial scandals give them good reason to make this "use it or lose it" choice? If instead of socking it away from their own incomes, they're counting on reaping a financial windfall when they inherit what the government, banks, insurance companies, pension plans and savings and loan institutions haven't already expropriated from their parents, will they be worse or better off?

Insurance companies have not succeeded, and in too many instances, haven't even tried to get the boomer turned on to the whole insurance concept. Until insurance companies give boomers cause to consider insurance in their financial planning, boomers aren't going to be the big purchasers. Besides, employers have taken on such a large chunk of both life and medical insurance responsibilities as "perks" for employees, the insurance industry is going to be hard put to devise strategies for boomers to add to what they already have as employee benefits. *Financial Services Week* noted in an article last year that boomers will continue to place insurance at the bottom of their financial lists. The reasons? Boomers spend their discretionary income on consumer goods, have been questioning investments made by insurance companies, and are wondering if such companies will be next to topple. Niels Christiansen, who serves the American Council of Life Insurance as managing director of research, says, "You can't extrapolate from past generations and assume the baby boomers will behave just as their parents did." Excuse a little back-patting, but it's great to have some experts agreeing with me!

When the boomers do inherit what's left of this wealth, what are they going to do with it? Is it reasonable to expect them to leave it where it is gaining some paltry interest, or is it more likely they'll take it out of lending institutions, cash in the stocks, bonds and insurance, and spend the way they are spending now?

Boomers may not then have cash in the vault, but at least they'll have the homes, cars and other high-end products they've bought and won't be left with zero bank balances and phony excuses of why their money has disappeared. Boomers may not be as thrifty as they should be or read all the financial pages available to them, but they're smart enough to define S & L as Steal & Loot.

Take a look at what Alan Farnham wrote in May of 1990 in Fortune, when he refers to "the biggest intergenerational transfer of wealth in U.S. history." To quote Farnham, when the aging parents of today's boomers die, as much as "$6.8 trillion will . . . fall into the waiting laps of the kids." He notes that experts see some significant changes on the horizon, even if they don't all agree on what will happen. The influx of such large estates out of savings institutions and into the economy will have a noteworthy effect. Consumer debt could be retired; consumer spending could increase, and dramatically. Savings should soar, but perhaps not nearly as much as projected. The tax collectors may be waiting in the wings to legislate themselves extra large slices of the inherited pie. However the wealth is distributed and redistributed, profound changes in marketing strategy by every industry will be crucial.

The realization that this financial windfall is coming has already prompted many articles. One of the best appeared in last May's *U.S. News World Report*. In addition to the interesting case histories of how inherited wealth impacts recipients, there are some well-reasoned suggestions on "How Children Can Handle Their Windfalls." The first suggestion is one cautioning the nouveau riche not to squander the wealth, and to give considered thought before going into business for themselves. It continues with some thoughts on debt retirement, the pros and cons of paying off the mortgage, and some worthwhile savings methods for conserving the inheritance for themselves and their children. The September '91 issue of *The Boomer Report* discusses the issue of boomers and their spending. There are three important comments to be made. Yes, boomers will be making more in the year 2000, but also remember that echo boomers will be living at home and spending more of their parents' money than ever before. Also, it is important to note that the 45 to 55-year old male boomer will be influenced by his younger peers and therefore spending more for family and friends who are 25 to 34 years old!

An influx of funds of such magnitude is going to have far-reaching effect, and I read a number of books and articles on the subject. My advice to boomers? You are smart enough to make decisions in your own best interest. You are also clever enough to learn from experts, and discerning enough to recognize a con when you see one! Remember to keep one hand on your wallet.

To give a little credit, some banks and other lending institutions did try in the '80s to revise their marketing and advertising strategies to reach boomers and get them to save. But they never got into the boomer mind-set and failed miserably. According to some reports, fewer than 25% of banks with special package membership programs included components geared even to the older boomer, much less the younger. Most of them made the serious mistake of looking at boomers the way they've always viewed their aging depositors. They counted on boomers to fall into the same patterns as their more future-conscious parents. They forgot they were dealing with potential customers who think "now" and not "then."

Although financial marketing and advertising strategists said they recognized boomers as a different breed that had to be treated differently, they continued with the same tired methods in all of their efforts. No significant or far-reaching changes were made in advertising approaches, whether it was radio, newspaper, television, other print media or direct mail.

What appealed to those 55+ savings customers, and what appeals to the rest of the older population, does not and will not appeal to today's boomer, and that's true for the younger and older members of this increasingly affluent segment of the population. Their mind-set is "spend" and not "save." And it's going to take a supreme advertising and marketing effort to change that mind-set.

I addressed this issue in my rebuttal letter that appeared in the September '91 "Open Mike" column of *Broadcasting*. I was responding to a prior article explaining how to increase bank deposits by going after the older customer, and how to snag the boomer customer via car loans. Agreed, car loans are important to the boomers, but even the best-paid boomer may be finding it a tight squeeze to amass enough for a down payment on a first home. The financial institution that considers this and creates innovative plans leading to home ownership will capture a chunk of the lending market that will be the envy of his competitors. Such lending businesses will need to reexamine their own proclivities to see homebuying as an exercise only for the married couple. More and more, I'm placing some chips on the square that pays off for home loans to one or more persons wanting to build equity in real property regardless of whether they're married to anyone or each other! There's a message here for the home building industry thrown in gratis! Builders may need to "rethink" how they plan their structures to take into consideration the fact that they may be occupied by unrelated persons, each needing his or her own "space." Banks and other financial institutions should have started going after the boomer years ago because boomers are the spenders regardless of whether they have "discretionary" income or not! If you pay heed to what follows, you'll see that having money, at least for a good chunk of the boomers, just isn't going to be a problem.

In 1991, the first of the boomers hit age 45, and by doing so, started the projected increase in the number of households headed by those 45 to 54 years old. By the year 2000, that will have jumped a whopping 51%, and will mean 21.6 million boomers, the young-looking and young-acting "middle-aged" will be neatly slotted in peak earning years. *Business Week* got a firm grip on the boomer earnings situation in its *"How the Next Decade Will Differ"* article in September '89. It stated, "Indeed, the 1990s could turn out to be a period of extended economic prosperity. The baby-boom generation, highly educated, with two decades of work experience under its belt, is reaching peak productivity."

Recessions do have the side effect of encouraging savings,

and there has been a slight increase in the amount Americans set aside. For the boomer, the preferred option appears to be 401(k) employee plans that offer compound interest. When employers sweeten the pot by adding a percentage in matching funds, even boomers who like spending better than saving could sit up and take notice. And those pension plans go a long way toward establishing loyalty to a company, something job-switching boomers are not especially prone to have. Many financial analysts see emerging hints that older boomers are socking a bit more under the mattress. Larry Chambers, author of <u>The First Time Investor</u>, predicts an upswing in the savings rate by at least 20% in the next ten years. He believes boomers will lead the rush to save as they begin to see the need to prepare for retirement.

How many of you found your piggy bank raided by your folks when you were kids? There seems to be some pretty convincing evidence that echo boomers will be showing mom and dad the way to squirrel some coins away. Echo boomers are spenders like their parents, but findings show they are also savers like their grandparents. A financial report issued a few years ago told of the $2.6 billion children aged four to twelve had in their savings accounts. Hey, I don't want to see a return of the depression, believe me, but I wouldn't be astonished to hear boomers saying, "Daughter (or son), can you spare a dime?"

Goldman Sachs and Company issued reports of studies that certainly appear to support my view of boomers as spenders, not savers. It's not that boomers totally reject the idea of saving, it's that some of them, in the lower income brackets especially, spend more than they make and can't save. Others, who already have teens entering college, spend every extra dime on those school costs. Those in the higher financial echelons are not expected to increase their savings percentages either. Experts don't agree on what all this means, but they do admit lower savings leads to lower economic growth. This, combined with a national debt that just keeps on growing, doesn't paint a rosy picture of America's financial future.

Peter Kerr, writing for the *New York Times News Service,* concluded his article about marketing changes and concerns about possible future money problems with a great line that bears repeating. He was quoting Rutgers University Professor James Hughes who said, "The generation that was once associated with dropping acid in order to escape reality is now going to be dropping antacid in order to cope."

A few months ago, a poll by the Gallup Organization came up with some interesting, but inconclusive findings. In a survey of 1,000 boomers older than 30, in households earning more than $30,000 annually there was an indication that some of those boomers are starting to make plans for the time when they leave the work force. But they were in the income brackets where there is a tad left over at the end of every pay period so something can be set aside.

Time will tell. Our country's track record for percentage of income saved isn't very good when compared to other major industrial countries.

Researchers are already very much interested in what boomers will do after the big "R" day has come. *The Boomer Report* of June 15, '91, gives a preview based on the Gallup survey of what might happen. Travel and vacations are on the agenda for 88%. Of the 41% who said they would relocate, 40% are heading for warmer climes. It won't be retirement for 9%, as they plan to continue working full-or part-time. Civic, charitable and cultural institutions will benefit from the volunteer work planned by 8%. "Fore" will be a favorite word for the 7% who plan to play a lot of golf. The sporting industry can look for some 5% to hang the "Gone Fishing" sign on their doors, and craft shops will appreciate the 4% who'll be involved in unnamed hobbies.

In that same issue, other economic indicators showed some changes in 1990 boomer savings habits to show this group is at least beginning to think about retirement planning. The results, however, were called "curious." The upturn expected because of the Persian Gulf War just did not materialize, and real estate pages all over the country were noting a slump. I don't know about you, but I'll be watching for other more definitive signals to help me advise my clients.

"The Coming World Labor Shortage" appeared in an issue of *Fortune* last year. Louis S. Richman discussed the "demographic San Andreas fault" he believes is threatening the United States, Japan and Europe with an economic earthquake because there will be too few workers after the year 2000. Although absolute numbers of births are high, birthrates here and elsewhere have been falling to below the average 2.1 per woman of childbearing age. In our country, that's the number needed just to stay even, he writes. Solutions for this problem are varied, and include delaying retirement, permitting more immigration, and improving productivity and education so that fewer workers can produce more.

Complicating the projected labor shortage are some dismal statistics about high school dropout rates, births to unmarried and/or teenaged mothers, and poverty.

As far as the older worker goes, I'm betting many who retired while still healthy and active will return to the work force in large numbers. Using our own resource pool of qualified senior citizens may well make the difference in our nation's ability to compete with the rest of the world.

Edwin Chen, writing for the *Los Angeles Times* this

summer said, "American demographers are excited about what they foresee as a unique period of prosperity in the next two decades, as the third of the population known as the baby boomers reaches early middle age, the peak years of productivity and earnings."

Among his interesting observations were the possible return to work by retired persons, either in low-paying jobs or as entrepreneurs starting their own businesses; the possible decline in the growth of the fast food industry, and a significant change in vacation habits.

Those "hard-hitting careers" I mentioned are beginning to look to some as if they're in industries configured like funnels. There are a great number of jobs, and good ones at that, at the wide end. But when that funnel narrows, look for a great deal of boomer soul-searching if that expected promotion isn't offered. I differ with the experts who say boomers will begin to doubt themselves. Boomers will be more likely to doubt the abilities of upper management who didn't plan adequately and expand their business domain so there would be "plenty of room at the top." I submit that boomers are, and will continue to be, a self-assured, self-confident generation.

This entire issue of "plateauing," reaching a certain level in one's profession and then getting stuck there, is a fascinating one. Look for more books and articles dealing with this concern. I confess I'm still mulling the issue. Hasn't it always been historically true there are fewer workers at the top than in the middle? Some boomers are obsessed with rocketing to the top, with "making it." Some have reasonable expectations and are content with small, steady steps. Seems foolish to me for the experts once again to clump all boomers and expect the same reaction and the same behavior from each and every one of them.

Barbara Block, who writes on business and careers, has

made some significant observations about the decreasing number of opportunities she and others think exist at the pinnacle of success. While I think ambitious boomers will make their own pinnacles, I agree Ms. Block has some thought-provoking things to say.

If the truly hard-working boomer doesn't reap all the rewards coming to him or her, outlets for that frustration will become necessary. Turning to other areas for satisfaction, to families, volunteer work and hobbies, as Ms. Block suggests, provides some of the answers. I contend boomers will come to grips with the "too many people, too few jobs" situation. Due to the fact they are stressed because they *didn't* get the whopping raise, or stressed because they *did,* they'll be needing more relaxation away from the rodent run! And that, again, points out the need for individualized marketing efforts. Clever advertisers and marketers will make it because they know boomers don't fall into the same mode just because of their numbers. They have unique profiles.

Savings industries are going to have to realize that in order to be successful in this and subsequent decades, they are going to have to understand boomers don't see saving as the value their parents saw. Even though we know that as people get older they see security in their older years as more of a value than they did when they were younger, we have to remember we are dealing with boomers—whom many correctly view as the adult *teenage* population! Until the banking industry gets that through its thick skull, it is going to be in deep trouble for the rest of this decade and beyond.

Let's take into consideration that 80% of all the current savings accounts belong to people who are older than 55 right now. So the banking industry and the savings and loans are already in deep trouble because boomers are so under-represented. 70% of all mortgage-free homes in the United

States are owned by the 60+ group. These statistics are from the banking industry itself; it should be apparent to them that the boomer population is the one that needs attention, not the so-called Golden Agers who have long since completed their future planning and who already own their homes.

According to *The Boomer Report* of December 1989, boomers at present consume 51% of all goods and services in this country. I hate to stress the fact that the publication's same issue also pointed out that bankers needed to go after the boomer quickly, but by and large they still haven't gotten the message. Only a few in the industry have offered special packages for the 30+ crowd, something that has to take place in order to get the boomers used to saving their money in banks. If the banks and other like institutions don't wake up and smell the coffee, they are going to be in worse trouble than they are now.

The boomers' spending power is going to soar 90% between now and the year 2000. The number of households headed by 30 to 50-year-olds with incomes of more than $50,000 will triple during the same period. Right now, some 80% of boomers have credit cards and more than a third of those will charge at least $1,000 during the next twelve months. Only a small number of banks and other like institutions recognize that the boomer has grown up using or seeing credit used. More and better credit products will have to be offered to take advantage of this trend, and those programs, surprisingly enough, will need to be developed for the older population as well. The boomer influence reaches both forward and back! Financial institutions need to take a very serious look at these spending patterns, and they have to begin immediately.

Something else that needs to be addressed and capitalized upon is the fact that it is the younger banking customer who uses automated teller services. At the very least, that should alert banking officials to know that efficient and *fast* service is desired by the younger customer. Build in speedy and more computerized services for the boomer consumer, and acceptance of those services is more likely to occur.

Another issue they need to examine, and quickly, is the growing financial influence of working women boomers. As of 1977, more than 58% of women worked outside of the home. By 1995, that figure should reach 80%, according to *The Boomer Report*. A new profile must be developed for this customer. Creative strategies need to be put into action expanding the customer base to concentrate effort on the emerging controllers of the most resources, and that certainly means women boomers as well as their male counterparts.

I'm not saying ignore the existing older customer. What I am saying is that they are becoming the minority and need to be replaced by new boomer customers. And not only will marketing and advertising strategies have to change, those in charge of making these changes will have to understand that even among boomers there are different approaches that will need to be taken.

Those on the younger end of the boomer scale are just now moving into well-paying jobs and don't have much going for them—yet. But as we approach the 2000s, this larger group will be increasingly entering into the higher-earnings brackets now occupied by the older boomer. At the same time, the older boomers will be getting ready to retire. Talk about the need for different and unique marketing and advertising strategies!

Boomers will not automatically become savers unless they are motivated and rewarded. And they will have to be reminded to save more often. This holds true for all types of advertising and marketing. Boomers will only react to offers of combined banking and non-banking services that take their special needs and interests into consideration, and those packages must be targeted to and geared towards this large, unique group of potential savers. If this group doesn't use financial services, in a short time, who will be left that will use them?

All I can say for financial institutions out there is don't even bank on the boomers coming into your fold unless you go into theirs.

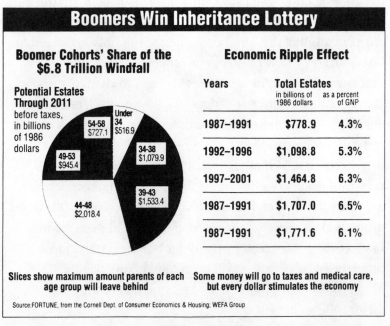

Boomers Win Inheritance Lottery

Boomer Cohorts' Share of the $6.8 Trillion Windfall

Potential Estates Through 2011
before taxes, in billions of 1986 dollars

- Under 34 $516.9
- 54-58 $727.1
- 34-38 $1,079.9
- 49-53 $945.4
- 39-43 $1,533.4
- 44-48 $2,018.4

Slices show maximum amount parents of each age group will leave behind

Economic Ripple Effect

Years	Total Estates in billions of 1986 dollars	as a percent of GNP
1987–1991	$778.9	4.3%
1992–1996	$1,098.8	5.3%
1997–2001	$1,464.8	6.3%
1987–1991	$1,707.0	6.5%
1987–1991	$1,771.6	6.1%

Some money will go to taxes and medical care, but every dollar stimulates the economy

Source:FORTUNE, from the Cornell Dept. of Consumer Economics & Housing; WEFA Group

Chart reprinted from **The Boomer Report**

CHAPTER 6

Echo Boomers

May the bough never break and the cradle never fall

Now that "Rock-a-bye baby" has become one of the rock 'n' roll boomer generation's top hits, what kind of parents will boomers be to their echo boomer children? What guidance can they give based on their experience as the most-studied population on the face of this whirling planet? Will they pass on some of the positives, or have the events boomers faced colored their outlooks so negatively they won't be able to promise a glowing future to their precious progeny?

Take heart. Focus study groups adequately show that boomers are taking their roles as parents more seriously than anything else. Marketers speak about "top of the mind." Well, for many boomers, children take the undisputed place. The double-income couple of the recent past may still have two healthy paychecks each month, but now they are thinking of stashing a chunk away to benefit their kids. While they used to run out of money before they ran out of month, increasingly boomers are planning ahead to give their children the same, if not more, benefits that they received.

To the extent they can swing it, boomer couples are moving into homes of their own, and see the growing equity in these homes as the safety net that might provide the money needed to educate their children. Home improvement is a booming industry, and boomers may well be planning ahead to accommodate the echo boomers with living space even *after* they complete college.

Agreed, the mind-set of the boomers is to think and act young for the rest of their lives, but that sure doesn't mean they are ignoring the important issues that face them as parents. Because they rebelled against everything as children, and suffered a communications gap with the very people who could have taught them growing up and growing old are natural parts of the life process, they were tuned out. Boomers find it difficult, perhaps impossible, to fully accept aging in their own minds, and many seem to share the view *they'll* never grow old. Staying young with their own children might be the answer.

Please understand, though, that when I say boomers will be teenagers for the rest of their lives, I don't mean they are an immature generation. They just like to play like big kids. And, if successes of the repeat showings in movie houses and on videotape mean anything, boomers sit right down with the kids to watch their old favorites from Disney Studios. It's not by accident that newer movies seemingly made for the sandbox set have dialogue only an adult can "get."

In spite of this somewhat unrealistic attitude that sees rock 'n' roll in the future, not rocking chairs, boomers are indicating a desire to avoid "gaps" between them and their children. In fact, the lines between boomer parent and echo boomer child are becoming less and less distinct. Through the years, of course, it's been natural to expect parents and children to share some interests, but nowadays, except for the obvious age difference, you can't tell one from the other. In the March '91 *The Boomer Report* there are two tiny articles that point out some interesting facets of the boomer longing for their childhood with huge doses of nostalgia, something some experts see as fascinating for the "Now" generation. When old favorite Crayola colors were retired to be replaced by bright neons of the '90s, some boomers were so upset they actually joined a group pressing for the return of the old colors. Favorite cartoon characters, that one might expect to pop up everywhere for the kiddies, are also in vogue among the boomers. Cases in point? Executives sporting Mickey Mouse suspenders, cartoons on bank checks, and, one of the nuttiest, one boomer's attache case is really a Marvel Comics lunch box!

Classic toys are being snapped up by boomers who whoop with delight if they find an original Barbie or G.I. Joe stashed in their parents' attics. You won't have to look far for ads capitalizing on the nostalgia craze. Consumer research has uncovered what some of us knew all along. Boomers love recalling their childhood, so we'll all be treated to repeat performances of ads, jingles and slogans of the '50s and '60s. What's more, in case you haven't noticed, some of those ads are in catchy black and white. You'll see dad and mom happily playing with new models of old favorite electric trains, and Lincoln Logs will again find an honored place in front of the yule log blazing away in the fireplace.

Worry warts who must have a great deal of time on their

hands are concerned that boomers are spending too much energy trying to recapture their pasts and not enough on dealing with today's problems. How do I feel about it? If boomers could survive the turbulent '60s, and they have, I am confident they'll manage to handle problems presented to them today and tomorrow.

They wear the same clothes, listen to the same music, make important decisions together and enjoy many of the same activities. It's important, though, to question the underlying reasons for this shared behavior. To me, it's just more reinforcement that boomers are not going to grow creaky without a good battle to stay hearty. Even if some are acting like kids to avoid facing the fact they haven't really found that elusive fountain of youth, deep inside they know *acting* young isn't actually *being* young. But *feeling* young is another story.

Last year, I went to the Paul McCartney concert in Berkeley, California. I looked around and saw some spectacular sights. First of all, the lights in the stadium were blacked out and there were 60,000 boomers and their kids there. When Paul started singing about peace and the environment, 40,000 butane lighters lit up at one time. I looked around and saw boomers who were 35, 40, and even older, dressed the same way they were thirty years earlier at Haight-Ashbury in San Francisco. At that point, absolutely no one could tell me I was not looking at the adult teenage population.

The boomlet generation numbered 42 million by 1989, and, in spite of a lowered birthrate, this tally of newcomers will grow substantially in the '90s. Not every boomer woman will have children; many will have only one, but the number of boomer women contributing to the baby population is still large, and won't fully diminish until early in the next century.

Echo boomers will reflect their boomer heritage not just demographically but psychographically: these kids are spenders just like their parents. So marketing to the boomlet—the Echo Generation—has a lot in common with selling to the boomers. Partly because many boomers postponed having children, such families will continue to dominate the marketplace well into the future through the sheer force of their numbers. Sharp marketers know that older parents are quite probably in a more secure financial position and naturally want top-of-the-line merchandise for their kids.

A number of interesting factors about echo boomers are coming to light. Demographers have noted that many of these children will grow up in households with no siblings. Other experts point out the plusses and minuses of growing up alone. There is the obvious benefit that family resources don't have to be stretched as far, and only children will have more parental attention and more goodies. Only children benefit from being the first in a lot of areas—no hand-me-downs, for one. The fact that there are so many first children and only children currently being born makes for happy cash registers. Babies, as any parent who has two brain cells to rub together knows, need a lot of "stuff." And that stuff is coming with price tags that make the less affluent cringe. However, only children often have to live up to the lofty expectations of their doting parents, and that can lead to psychological problems when kids just can't cut the mustard.

Scholarly studies, both now and in the past, have also discovered some patterns concerning birth order. Children born first often do better in school than subsequent kids do, but they also bear heavier responsibilities and are expected to play pretty grown-up roles in the family. As echo boomers grow older, they are going to be facing many of the same problems their boomer moms and dads faced. The numbers game will be replayed, albeit on a smaller scale, and these kids, too, will face crowded schools and limited job opportunities.

Skim through the financial magazines and this is what you'll find. "Advertisers are falling all over themselves to reach the nation's 32 million kids between ages 4 and 12." That statement appeared in the respected *Forbes* magazine in 1990. *Adweek* told us "Advance sales of ad time for kids-TV hit a record of $450 million in 1990, up 25% from 1989." Advertising should really hit home with these children who influence almost 80% of the buying decisions.

Academics doing their research have been finding that advertisers are targeting messages to children, even when the small fries are known not to be consumers of the products and services in question. James McNeal, professor of marketing at Texas A&M, found that to be the case and discussed it in <u>Children as Consumers</u>.

Magazines written for children boast advertisers that one would expect to see only in publications geared to the adult market. Also pointed out by Forbes is the somewhat less than altruistic means companies are using to get children to recognize their brand names. Many provide free teaching materials to schools, and you can bet those donors have their logos prominently displayed. I'm not saying this is bad—it serves some excellent purposes for corporations to help students. What I am saying is that it's yet another indication of the role children play and how important they are to reach. Who can resist some little moppet begging for an Apple computer or a Polaroid camera? And, if the product they want boomer mom and boomer dad to buy has an educational purpose, well, that purchase is as good as made. Education continues to be important to the boomers; it will be important to them that their children are not neglected in this area.

Advertisers are well aware that spending last year for and by the 12-years-old and-younger set topped $75 billion. Believe it or not, kids of this age already boast personal, annual incomes totalling $9 billion. The economy may be slow, but not in the area of spending on the little tykes. Purchases made by and for children aged 4 to 12 jumped 25% in 1989, according to *Forbes* magazine. Remember I've mentioned just about everyone in the U.S. wants to be perceived as younger than they are? The exceptions to the rule are kids. Marketers are advised to go after kids a few years older than their true target market. Babies *are* cute, but if kids think something is babyish, you may as well pitch the campaign into the nearest litter container.

A better item to pitch is the value of kids themselves when it comes to learning about products and services they'll ask for or buy for themselves. A few years ago, Polaroid used a consulting team of kids. These precocious potential purveyors of products came up with an idea for a new model of camera that netted the company a cool $15 million!

There may be a recession, but by and large, it hasn't hit businesses producing goods and services for babies and kids. Upscale items, including an infant car seat with a remote control to rotate it in a full circle, and a pram that costs a thousand bucks, are doing well. Companies are targeting the small fries, and very effectively, to turn them into consumers. The kids now even have their own pint-size shopping carts to zip around many supermarkets with mom and dad. Has it escaped your notice that play areas are being added to malls, grocery stores and fast-food restaurants? I've said that boomers want to play like big kids, but it's their children who have become the target market and who now get to play almost wherever they go.

Echo boomers are certainly the lucky ones when it comes

to the "try-before-you-buy" concept now becoming more and more popular in toy shops. Giant retailers have the dollar edge, but more and more of the smaller stores are giving children the chance to touch and play with items these retailers know the kids will ask to have. Shopping malls are adding a number of toy shops that have become fun havens for parents weary of a day of shopping. For the kids, such places are wonderlands. Recall the "don't touch" mentality of the past, and how frustrated you felt when you were not allowed to handle the merchandise? Today, echo boomers not only handle it, they practically tell toy makers what they want—and they get it! And upscale parents don't mind shelling out a few extra shekels to pay for the toys and the fun kids have in the kiddie kingdoms.

Food marketers have been in the vanguard of the enlightened and awakened. Have you ever in your life, aside from breakfast cereals, seen a wider array of food products for children? Some of the swifter marketers include games and little toys right in with packaged foods so the tykes can be entertained while mom or dad slaves over a microwave. Products come in kid-sized portions, and the names on some of the packages are destined to be the ones these miniature consumers ask their parents to buy. Catch this from *The Boomer Report* of December 1990 in an article discussing buying for the echo boomers, "McCain Ellio's Teenage Mutant Ninja Turtle Pizza contains no turtles (or teenagers) but is selling briskly."

Parents, mothers especially, may feel they're short-changing their families by not producing gourmet delights from scratch. Manufacturers of food products know of this "guilt," and are making it easier and easier to serve fairly decent meals by the double whammy of appealing to the kids and to the short-of-time parent who cooks for the family. Did you think food manufacturers were going to ignore the yearning for the good old days? Not on a bet. Adults are now the stars on breakfast food commercials, and not many of us have missed the "how to open and eat an Oreo cookie" ad.

Try an experiment to prove the impact of these echo boomers. Scan your television channels, leaf through a newspaper or magazine, and listen to the radio. While there is no absence in print or video of the slinky hard-body draped over the hood of a car she is suggesting you purchase, there is the noticeable presence of the adorable little cherub sitting in a tire. The sultry feminine voice used on radio to sell you something has been joined by the lisping exhortations to buy voiced by tiny tots. Believe me, folks, babies are in. And you'll notice more and more of them becoming part of your favorite sitcoms, acting as well as selling.

I promised to give you some more information on my association with FOX Broadcasting Company, so here it is! FOX has made the wise decision to reach both boomer parents and their echo boomer youngsters with sharp, innovative, new programs—programs more than a little out of the ordinary. Programs that, in fact, recognize that these two groups are also a bit out of the ordinary. Where in the past FOX saved its big guns for the fall, now it spreads the new programming around over the entire year.

One might ask, why has this network chosen to go after this market? Don't the oldsters have control of this nation's spending cash? If FOX executives believed this, they wouldn't be delivering to advertisers what many of them are finding to be the solid economic benefit of boomer buyers! FOX has also recognized an interesting difference between boomer kids and their folks. Where boomers exhibit very little brand loyalty, boomer kids show a great deal of it. FOX notes in addition that the echo boomers serve their parents and peers as early warning systems. They note the trends, and even fuel them. I can't think of any advertisers who'll complain about that. It's like having an unpaid sales force working for them every time the dial is switched to FOX. Actually, though, "unpaid" is a misnomer. FOX viewers are getting programs they like, and quite correctly see that as a fair bargain.

On the plus ledger, though, boomers are closer to their children, and really don't want another generation gap like they had with their parents. Because they portray themselves as cool parents, their kids want to be like them. And make no bones about it, boomers *love* being seen as cool, because that's another indication they are still young. Boomers who were turned off to their parents don't want their children turned off to them. They want to be known as the kind of parents their parents weren't, and to a large degree, boomers can and do relate to the younger generation much better than their parents did to them.

For the flip side, I was amused by an article by Harry Shearer in *Los Angeles Times Magazine* last February. "The Generation Rap: The Baby-Boom Bunch Has Begun to Belittle the Brains of Its Heirs," aimed a few well-chosen arrows at what some boomers think about the younger generation. He asserts that most parents are proud of their own kids, but other people's whelps are just not to be believed. In what sound like reverberations from the past, Shearer finds adults are not at all sure the younger generation is worthy to inherit the earth. Boomers describe other people's kids as "anarchists, conformists, lazy good-for-nothings or materialistic greedheads." On a serious note, he finds it lamentable that adults blame the kids for their failings, and asks the question: "After all, who reared those monsters?"

For those who are stuck with the idea that all boomers are only interested in a quick trip to the executive suite, and don't spend time with their families, even in this harried, hurried world, boomers have dinner with their families at least five times a week. A way to solve what some refer to as the "time famine" would be welcomed by just about anybody, busy boomers in particular. Boomers have full calendars as they balance relationships, marriages, parenting, fitness training, and climbing the workplace ladder. Show them a product that will do it better, do it faster, and leave them time for their echo boomers, and you've got a sale.

Give them a service that provides some extra minutes, and you've found a winning combination for your success and for boomer repeat business. I ask you, do you know any boomer who can afford to "job it out" who doesn't? Time is money, but money is for spending to gain time to do things boomers like to do, not things they have to do. Come on, be honest, wouldn't you rather spend your precious time doing something fun, or do you really like changing the oil in your car?

Another somewhat startling finding comes from a 1989 survey by Robert Half International, an executive recruiting firm. It revealed that 74% of the boomer men interviewed preferred a "daddy track" job to a "fast track" job. To spend more time with their children, 45% said they were willing to do without the trappings of promotions. A popular hotel has cashed in on the desire for more "daddy track" jobs to allow more time to spend with the children. Ads show a boomer dad holding the hand of his little girl as they prepare to go swimming together after her first swimming lesson from, who else, the beloved daddy who has taken her (and the rest of the family) on a vacation.

There have always been pros and cons about whether or not married couples should avoid divorce and stick together for "the sake of the children." A *Washington Post* article early this year discussed this issue, and it's another one sure to get a lot of ink. According to the article, more and more family counselors are urging boomer parents to tough it out whenever possible. Sociological studies have long indicated that kids suffer the most from divorce and carry the psychological scars with them to school, where they have more problems than children in a stable family environment. Children of divorce are more likely to get divorced themselves.

When we turn the calendar pages to welcome 1995, and possibly even sooner, look out! Those who study statistics think we should be planning for an upsurge in all kinds of crime as a new crop of kids hits the late teens. Echo boomers, those born after the birthrate dip that followed the baby boom, are already finding themselves on the police blotter more often. It's not a new phenomenon for kids to perform well on the crime charts. Again it's arithmetic that will make the impact.

Experts expect the rate to continue to escalate, especially because the number of kids entering these crime-prone years keeps getting bigger. Sociologists are having a field day with these findings, and blame poverty and divorce for the surge. I hope the experts are wrong about this area, but I'm afraid they may, for once, be calling a shot correctly. I can't argue with the facts.

On the other side of the issue, many believe divorce is a too-handy scapegoat to blame for all of society's ills, and in many cases, view divorce as an appropriate solution. As there are so many boomer marriages ending up in front of the judge, keep your eye peeled for more developments on this front.

Because there are many more echo boomers than just about anyone predicted, profound changes are soon to occur in education and child care, two very significant areas of concern to boomer parents. Forty-two million of anything is a huge number, and when we're talking about providing important services for that many children, it's stratospheric!

At present, big commercial providers of child care take in a mere 4% of the money spent on this crucial service. Friends, neighbors, relatives and small, independent centers supply the rest. Parents are justifiably concerned about the horror stories they read every day about poor care, and worse, child abuse by care givers, and are willing to pay a few dollars more for assurances that their child will be safe and protected. I've been noticing numerous articles about a planned proliferation of day care chains. More babies were born in 1990, 4.2 million, than were born in any other year since 1957, and that year's 4.3 million number is engraved on my memory cells.

Federal guidelines and control of this industry are not far-fetched ideas, but as boomers hold fast to their quite understandable distrust of national leaders, and their desire for individual and more localized control, this wicket will be a sticky one, indeed. For what many fail to take into consideration is the fact that day care is crucially needed on both ends of the age spectrum. Our "sandwiched" boomers, caught in the middle between their parents and their children, are looking for quality care by compassionate professionals for their parents, and are seeking stimulating, loving care for their children at the same time.

Although the day care field is expensive, both to build as well as to attend, I expect an increase in their number and look for a substantial improvement in site planning. Salaries for day care workers have never been particularly high, but if it's true that more and more retired persons want to use their still youthful older years to make a contribution, if they truly do want to get back into the work force, perhaps that will serve as a partial solution.

Advertising Age ran a three-part series this summer, and devoted a full segment of its *Changing Markets* to "Wooing Boomers' Babies." The senior vice-president for marketing and strategic planning for Kinder-Care Learning Centers, John Kaegi, was quoted in that article. "We're seeing different parents than we served five years ago. We're serving clients that are 28 to 35—the second half of the baby boom. They are more pragmatic, less idealistic, and more stressed out." No wonder they're stressed out. Finding good day care for babies is difficult; finding great day care often means parents go on a waiting list and have to find stopgap measures. Such giants in the industry as Kinder-Care, the largest day care chain in the country, are often unable to accommodate every little patron. The article mentions a lottery had to be held for coveted spots at La Petite Academy's Washington, D.C. location when it opened.

Remember in the introductory chapter when I talked about how the boomers revolutionized the diaper industry? Echo boomers are causing a diaper revolution of their own. When the big bird delivered the boomer babies, parents had few decisions to make about what the new member of the family was going to wear from the waist down. It truly was one size fit all, in any color desired, as long as that color was white! What a difference a few years make. In today's world of designer fashion, choices abound for the pre-toddler set. Supermarkets and department stores offer an array of sizes, styles and patterns of cloth or paper britches, appropriately on the shelves in blue for him, pink for her. Disposable diapers are a $3.8 billion a year industry. Yes, there is a paradox here. Boomers have traditionally been concerned about the environment, but that hasn't halted sales of disposable diapers! Cloth diapers don't even come close at $60 million, with most sales to diaper services and only 20% to retail consumers. Babies born in the 1990s may well be eating Gerber baby food and wearing the cloth diapers the firm markets under its Gerber and Curity brands. New moms will be receiving "Bundle of Joy" flowers now that FTD, Florists Transworld Delivery and Gerber, the baby food giant , have joined forces. Fresh flowers will be delivered with non-food items and discount coupons from Gerber.

Newcomers have carved out a spot in the baby food market, partly by appealing to boomer parents' desire for wholesome, natural foods touted as organically grown. Those who purvey fast-foods to the older child and to adults are waiting in the wings rubbing their hands together in anticipation of the day when the toddler toddles into *his* emporium. And what will the pint-sized gourmet find? A menu meant just for kids will be prominently displayed at most fast-food places and, increasingly, at restaurants catering to those on a modest budget.

Think back to the last cocktail party you attended when a chic woman pulled out of her purse a huge portfolio of photographs she couldn't wait to show you. If you've been held captive by such a doting grandmother, you won't need three guesses to figure out who else is being targeted as a purchaser of clothes, toys and books for the sandbox set. Grandparents account for some 25% to 50% of the goodies purchased for kids, a fact not lost on toy makers such as Playskool and Mattel. *Advertising Age* tells us such manufacturers are doing well with their traditional product lines, but are also adding goodies for grandparents (and parents, too, of course) to purchase for the newly-arrived members of the baby boomlet. Look for more advertising appeals to grandma and grandpa, a market that many think has been neglected in the past.

Anyone who does any mall crawling at all surely has noticed the explosion in the kiddie clothing market and the profusion of new places to shop. Where once you found a children's section tucked away in a corner of a department store, there are now places by the dozen dedicated to togs for infants, toddlers and older children. The Gap chain has pulled off a marketing coup with its GapKids and BabyGap. Know what? A lot of the clothing looks pretty much like what the boomers themselves are wearing. It's been found that boomers are spending more money on their children than they are spending on themselves.

In another smooth marketing move, Sears, Roebuck and Company instituted a warranty program this summer that offers free replacement of a child's clothing if it wears out before it's outgrown. KidVantage covers apparel purchased in regular stores, and also carries with it some attractive discounts on future clothing purchases.

On to another major concern—education.

Education was of supreme importance to boomers; they will not see it as less so for their children. But when they start looking at the costs of sending Master and Missy Echo Boomer out to earn that coveted sheepskin, they may well begin to look for sensible, and less costly alternatives.

A hopeful sign is the rapid increase in the number of magazines published just for echo boomers and the skyrocketing sales of children's books in both hard cover and paperback versions. Boomers may not read, but those who were read to in pre-television days are sharing that experience with at least some of the kids in the new generation.

Sales of encyclopedias were projected to be high, and they are. Boomer parents are providing them for their children, and there are special versions for kids not much older than toddlers, as well as computerized versions of the popular teaching aid. Reading, arithmetic and drawing programs that are fun to use are popping into more and more home computer drives as children as young as two learn to boot the family 'puter. While there are valid arguments regarding the pros and cons of computer-aided learning, and whether information received without the interaction of teachers and peers will take, there is no question that the electronic age has reached the classroom and the home.

Gannett News Service is writing articles about the increasing popularity of the two-year college, once thought of as education's "orphan." Even the more affluent boomer parents may think about comparing costs, and use the two-year or four-year community colleges to get their progeny started along the higher educational path. For less than $1,000 a year, students can attend a two-year college. Four-year community colleges are somewhat more costly, with an average of $1,750 annually. Compare that to the whopping $7,700, it costs on the average for a four-year private school. (And you don't have to be a graduate of the London School of Economics to realize that's much lower than the price tag on Ivy League schools.)

Other approaches are being suggested for elementary schools as well. Again quoting from the Adele Malott interview with John Naisbitt and Patricia Aburdene, "One new area for privatization particularly intriguing for Naisbitt is America's education system, which he describes as one created for yesterday's era, for the industrial economy, instead of one designed for the global information economy."

Naisbitt believes alternatives to traditional schools would offer more variety, and would open a formerly closed system to the fresh air of competition. He sees the existing decentralization of educational districts as a plus, but believes

Chapter 6

more educational choice would be preferable, and would produce better educated Americans. (Speaking of education, troubling statistics and studies have emerged showing that although a larger percentage of people now attend college than in any previous generation, they aren't necessarily better schooled. SATs, Scholastic Aptitude Tests, those dreaded examinations developed to show whether or not one is college material, declined in every year since boomers came of age.)

I would relish seeing boomer parents get behind this idea, and with their love of innovation and the resurgence of entrepreneurial spirit, perhaps they will.

Something that keeps on nagging at me is the reluctance on the part of a growing number of "experts" to understand that boomer attitudes about growing up and growing old are being reflected by the generation that followed them and by their children. *Newsweek*'s special edition, "The 21st Century Family," included an article bemoaning the fact that many post-boomer teens are "Young Beyond Their Years." Author Kenneth Woodward tells about over-indulged teens who "want to do everything sooner—everything but grow up." No blankety-blank wonder! Maybe they learned some life lessons too well from watching the boomers around them.

August '91 *Working Woman* featured an article dealing with some of the troubling attitude problems of what's referred to as "the twenty something generation." Boomer-age managers are having to deal with younger members of the work force, and they are finding those "kids" to be a bit much to handle. There is an increasing lack of respect for authority, questions about why management gets to make all the decisions, and a slightly askew view of their own value to the work force. These "baby busters" are equally as well-educated as boomers were, but because their numbers are so much smaller, they feel the job arena will be opening wide to them in just a few years, and boy, do they think they're ready right NOW! The writer, Katherine Ann Samon, points out that boomer bosses find it hard to deal with young employees partly because they exhibit some of the same characteristics common to the boomer. An observation made by Ms. Samon may hearten working moms. One of the reasons these cocky youngsters got that way is because both of their parents worked while they were growing up and they had to become more self-reliant to cope.

In the same magazine's September '90 issue, in Debra Kent's article, "Beyond Thirtysomething," she mentions that boomers are demanding the same kind of respect the newcomers are seeking. She makes the excellent point that "boomers will make the best employees because they'll be more skilled than succeeding generations." If that doesn't prove that echo boomers need some attention, nothing does. Education of this new generation is going to stretch the minds and resources of boomers and non-boomers alike. These children will need more skills, not fewer.

History tells us that parents throughout the ages have been convinced the next generation won't amount to anything. And each group of parents has been partly right, partly wrong. It is my hope that the special bonds that exist between boomer parents and boomer children will be strengthened by shared experiences and tempered by maturity as both groups strive for the best that life can offer.

Boomlet Births

in Millions

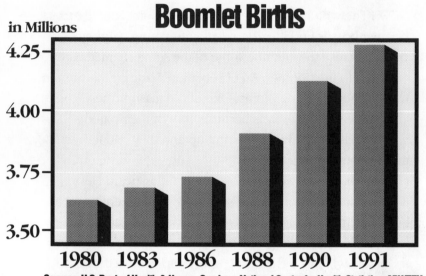

Sources: U.S. Dept. of Health & Human Services; National Center for Health Statistics; ADWEEK

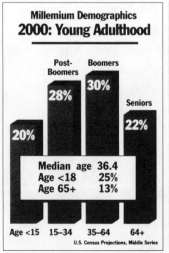

Millemium Demographics
2000: Young Adulthood

Post-Boomers 28%
Boomers 30%
Seniors 22%
20%

Median age 36.4
Age <18 25%
Age 65+ 13%

Age <15   15–34   35–64   64+
U.S. Census Projections, Middle Series

Post-Boomers vs. Boomers
How their attitudes differ

Post-Boomers	Boomers
Change as norm	Expect stability, security
Limits, frustration	Accumulation, growth
Coping, adaptation	Experimentation
Skepticism, ambivalence	Optimism, entitlement
Self-sufficiency	Do your own thing
Success=security against loss	Success=more, self-indulgence
Relationships: ambivalent, out-of-synch	Relationships negotiable

Conde Nast Survey

*Chart reprinted from **The Boomer Report***

CHAPTER 7

The Woman Boomer

Post-Macho Syndrome (PMS)
Backlash of the Brash Pack

First there was Eve. Then there was Gloria Steinem. What happened in between is a vague fairy tale about men ruling the world. Yes, of course women have historically had a hard time indeed, but at some significant moment in the late '60s, it became apparent that there was soon going to be almost no point in being male anymore. Not only would men cease to rule the world, they were going to be overruled and in some cases, ruled out altogether. The female boomer along with the attendant sociology of that one decade of the '60s were to change history.

However, the entire movement that was originally orchestrated to liberate women from their emotional and financial dependency, instead became the process whereby men actually became free to abandon the breadwinner role. While the female boomer fired up her self-absorbing unrelenting drive to run her own life, she muddied up the already convoluted relationship issues for all women forever more.

Not only did the American boomer woman burn her bra in the '70s, she also burned her bridges behind her. The very idea of living her mother's dream of wearing pearls to serve her family a heart-shaped meat loaf became a nightmare to this new woman.

Hers was the first generation of women who had access to the Pill. She finally had some measure of control over her body and certainly no one would mark her ballot for her. She voiced her opinion on the war, on Nixon, and on the "Mary Tyler Moore Show." Doubts about her subservient suburban role began to darken her perspective. Some critics of feminism say that her self-fixation heralded the end of the family as we once knew it.

But it was also the beginning of the mixed message that continues to plague women today. Women still fight the unspoken mandate that they be selfless, intelligent, sophisticated and servile while they seek their fortune in the male-dominated workplace. This contradiction, which will continue as long as we have two sexes, will shape our families' future and shape commerce as well. Once again, it all simply translates into marketing strategy.

Because women were changing their expectations about life and marriage, they were less likely to settle down. They were choosing to have fewer children, and they were having them later. They could now attend West Point for the first time ever. The term Ms. became more than just a new magazine. As though it were a sign of some cosmic order of things, on the fiftieth anniversary of women's suffrage in 1970, eighteen-year-olds were given the right to vote. Men were going to take a back seat to their wives, sisters, and now even their children.

Things were moving fast. And there was no turning back for The Woman. She was a living contrast to her older sister's inertia of the early '60s. She had marched for all sorts of "rights." Now she was marching herself right into the workplace to become one of the greatest sociological forces ever to shape our economy. By the '70s, 40% of all married women were employed. Females still only made about 65% of what their male counterparts did, but that gap would continue to be whittled down. Imagine what this did to men!

As sex roles became blurred, confusion was the norm. The war between the sexes was bitterly fought with no truce in sight. Cynicism, inflation and unemployment were key words and thoughts. Divorce rates soared, single-parent families were on the rise and those charming parlor rules existed only to be challenged. This incredible whirlwind of psychodrama spirals down to the marketer's bottom line—women are deciding how to spend the money. She is woman; you'd better hear her roar!

Magazine journalist Mary Cassidy was asked how she felt about her role as the archetypical younger female boomer. She was clear in her definition of herself and her position as a consumer. She states, "Speaking from my experience, you can describe boomer children in one word—'opportunists.' I know because I'm one. My mother falls on the tail-end of the boomer spectrum and I'm 25—on the cusp of the boomer sign. But I've learned more than a thing or two, such as the golden rules of being a boomer child:

- If you want it, get it, but try to get it on sale.
- If you charge it, pay your bills on time.

- Save, but enjoy yourself. (This is the contradiction in terms that this book is all about.)
- When you buy, buy the best — it lasts longer.
- Work hard, but don't forget to play hard.
- If you have the chance to travel–go!!
- Plan for retirement–but if you can withdraw the money to buy a house, do it. Otherwise you may not have one for a long time.
- Regardless of your age, you can have anything you want — you just have to try.
- You only go around once, so get as much out of it as you can.

"As a boomer child, I've stretched those rules. By the time I finished college, I had a fully furnished house with only the best in electronics, clothes, furniture, etc. — with the credit card bills to prove it. I had traveled and was working hard to break into the business world.

"When I think about it more deeply, I believe that you have to take the chance when you have it, or else it may not come again: whether it's a great suit, a great job or a great trip. Nothing ventured, nothing gained. Female boomers have fewer barriers than their older boomer mothers had. I can work in whatever capacity I choose, and I believe I can make it to the top, too.

"At home, I make more decisions. I have more say, if not the majority of the say in many matters. The men I associate with also let me say more and do more–they respect and encourage that.

"Ultimately, my mother's boomer generation changed things for me. Their way of life is mine only more so. I like new music, but I listen to the music of their era too. I am open to new things. When I'm old, I'll be even more dynamic than my mother. I'll listen to hers, mine and my children's music.

I'll get the most out of life. God only knows how much my children will want...if there's anything left after my generation gets finished!"

Historically speaking, the breadwinner system was not a very rewarding system for women to live by. The rule was firm. No matter how bad the family's financial situation was, the pre-boomer woman didn't have enough learned skills or confidence to bring home enough money to support her family adequately. The economy belonged to the men. Therefore, these women didn't know what it meant to "shoot for the stars." The only way their modest dreams could come true was to marry the "right" man. The boomer woman, complete with her strong determination and stubborn independence, changed this way of life forever—never to return to the caveman mentality. Boomer women started using their skills to shoot beyond the stars and men soon began looking for the "right" woman.

This change from dependence to independence has not been an easy transition for women. For example, it's difficult for the older boomer woman to go back in time and do it right. The thought of competing with the young, ambitious "today" woman is scary. But this fear of failure does not match up to the drive and determination the older boomer woman has to make up for lost time.

She remembers or hears from her relatives how it was back then. Having babies was the rage during the post-war era. The accepted reality at that time was that true happiness for women came from marrying a successful man, having his babies, and moving to the suburbs. Women were becoming mothers at a younger age than ever before. The popular magazines praised young women for their maternal abilities and their enthusiastic attitudes toward domestic life, not to mention their role as cheerleaders for young husbands on the way up. But just take a look at women's magazines today! Articles on how to make your own bread have a little different meaning now.

It was considered unfeminine for women of the pre-boomer era to have a job and not a family. How simple it all was. Most young women dropped their little careers after the war to start families and let the soldiers take over real jobs and real paychecks. A woman was at her sexiest when she was barefoot and pregnant. If a woman was over thirty and without a husband, she was considered an old maid and appropriate for the workplace. Nowadays, a woman will wait until her career is well on its way before she even considers marriage. The swaggering young bucks are finally realizing that the sexiest thing about a woman is her mind. And they are scared.

Another aspect of this difficult transition is the fact that, now that mommy works full time, she can't always be in charge of the household duties. Her responsibilities and attention are now focused on her own work outside the family. Many "Superwomen" try to juggle the responsibilities both in and out of the home. Many of these women succeed in handling both responsibilities, but burn-out is often an issue once their new, exciting personal life, chock full of career goals, interferes with car pool. In spite of such difficulties, women continue to make headway in the financial decision-making which affects their families and their businesses.

Lesley Allison, wife, mother, attorney and CEO of a dynamic health care organization describes the "Superwoman" conundrum.

"In early adolescence, a woman guidance counselor took me aside and said, *'You can do anything!'* Instead of being buoyed by optimism, I felt drowned in responsibilities. The message I heard beneath the spoken words was 'Because you are the first female generation with real choice, *You must be everything.* You must live your mothers' dreams, fulfill your fathers' fantasies, exceed your brothers' ambitions, expand your sisters' aspirations and create a new way for your unborn children.' Would she had counseled us to choose between diapers and dictation!

"As I approach 40, my mid-life crisis is not characterized as it was for my mother by the plaintive query, 'Is that all there is?' For boomer women, the existential dilemma is 'When will it be enough?' For many of us weaned in the insatiable optimism of the 1950's, the answer may be 'Never.'

"As boomer women come of (middle) age, the appetite to 'have it all' may be refined. Smart marketers in the 1990s will stop peddling objects and activities that make our lives merely full and start offering environments and experiences that render them satisfying."

However, certain elements of this "new way" will never be salvaged. Many women in dual-career marriages are finding that their marriage is lacking the intimacy it once had. Boomer women are finding out that they have to take precious time out of their busy schedules to re-establish intimacy with their mates. This intimacy was much easier to maintain when the husband had a life and the wife didn't. Now that the woman has a life of her own, some of the energy that was once focused toward the family is now being focused toward her job. This causes an emotional strain on the marriage. Some husbands just need time to get used to the change but others will never understand or be willing to accept the independence their wives are trying to establish. The "good" wife that used to be waiting patiently for the chance to provide support and dinner for him when he got home is now looking for that same support herself.

The boomer male is in a quandary. His woman doesn't see the strength and career aggression in him that she saw in her dominant father. She was influenced by her father's success-oriented behavior while her husband was babied by his apron-clad mother. This creates the dilemma of all time, perhaps never to be resolved. Men do not live up to her expectations. He will never be as strong as her father—but wait—maybe she doesn't want him to be. If he opens a door for her, will she thank him demurely or knee him in the groin? The struggle is internal. She wants him to have all those characteristics of strength and ambition that her father had, yet she wants to take over. So, who's in charge here? Is there any wonder that the divorce rate is so high? How can this not affect our economy?

In the pre-boomer years, when a woman reached a particular age, certain behaviors were clearly defined for her. It was appropriate and accepted that she was considered over-the-hill at a certain point in her life. That attitude has changed with the improvement of the female image as a power to be reckoned with. There is no pride in being a kindly graying cookie-making grandmother. Instead, she has flown like the wind out of that empty nest into a weight-lifting class. The so-called "middle-aged" woman of today claims to feel better about herself both physically and mentally than she's ever felt before.

Obviously, one of the most important consumer groups in the year 2000 will be women over 40. The smart marketers need to realize that the traditional categories used to describe their aging audience no longer apply. Youth and middle age are extending further and further into what we earlier thought was old age. The connotation of elderly as applied to women is negative. It is acceptable for women of all ages to be considered youthful and desirable. It is acceptable for a woman to be whatever age she is and still choose from products and services originally designed for her granddaughter.

Chronology is out, especially for women. Midlife translates into freedom, not crisis. Turning 40 no longer has anything to do with turning gray. Instead, it's a new beginning. Freedom is the key—freedom to be like Jane Fonda. Nowadays, women are taking more responsibility for their bodies by exercising and keeping fit. If you ask most women, they'll say they feel much younger than they actually are. They are more active and physically fit than the pre-boomer woman ever dreamed of being. But marketers are still shortsighted in their product and service target thrust when they continue to pretend that only 20-year-olds are looking forward to a good life.

The new improved lifestyle image of the boomer women can translate into dollars for the smart marketer. Even though she may be a single parent or a newly-divorced 45-year-old struggling financially in an underpaid job, she is still satisfied with the idea of making her own financial choices.

Emerging from that pink collar ghetto is a steadfast, slightly angry group of women who want to be heard, and that slow but sure emergence has come to dominate the commercial scene. Those women are insisting that certain luxuries of life, such as financial decision-making, are for them as well as for their brothers. However, some deeply-imbedded values will never change. In the late '50s, Margaret Mead wrote about wasted female talent as a result of women choosing marriage and family over career in spite of higher education and equal aptitude. She believed that marriage had a negative effect on the female since her career aspirations, although ambitious, were to be forever sabotaged by her sociologically-inbred desire to please her family first and foremost.

The Ageless Generation 121

Although she wants that corner office with her name in brass on the door, the primary concern of most working mothers is not, and never will be, success in the workplace. The well-being of her children is still her first priority and she can make it all work, even if it kills her marriage: Remember, boomer women were raised by June Cleavers to believe that a woman's success is still measured by how happy and well-adjusted her children are. And so, while the old rules are wearing off the stone, Ms. Boomer is still frantically trying to do it all.

Even if society were to eliminate all economic barriers to her career success, the boomer woman continues to remain a prisoner of her own psychology. The years of deprivation and confinement cannot be overturned with one generation. But the fragmentation of the role of the female leaves a window for the smart salesman. Any marketer who wishes to reach the American boomer consumer family needs to follow the woman from her office straight to her country kitchen, that is, after her quick stop for a manicure and aerobics.

Although the stable economy and sanctity of marriage were significantly threatened by all the psycho-social elements of the '60s, job security as a mother will never be in jeopardy. Remember, we still call them "working mothers." We'll never say "working fathers."

Because that dynamic impact of the '60s continues to leave those sex roles in a fury of turmoil, men as well as women aren't sure what success means to them. The whole contemporary idea of men trapped in the "rat race" has the same ideology for women trapped in the "feminine mystique." At this point, all we really know is that women are the decision-makers like never before in the history of the country. They hold the nation's purse-strings. Woe to the marketer who doesn't respond to the female boomer needs!

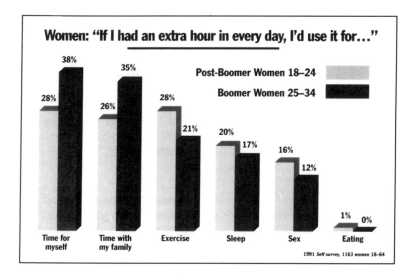

Women: "If I had an extra hour in every day, I'd use it for..."

Post-Boomer Women 18–24
Boomer Women 25–34

Time for myself	Time with my family	Exercise	Sleep	Sex	Eating
28% / 38%	26% / 35%	28% / 21%	20% / 17%	16% / 12%	1% / 0%

1991 *Self* survey, 1163 women 18–64

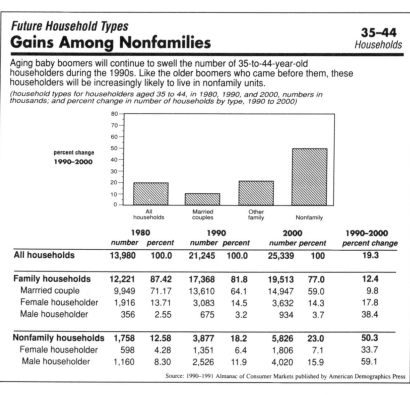

Future Household Types
Gains Among Nonfamilies

35–44
Households

Aging baby boomers will continue to swell the number of 35-to-44-year-old householders during the 1990s. Like the older boomers who came before them, these householders will be increasingly likely to live in nonfamily units.

(household types for householders aged 35 to 44, in 1980, 1990, and 2000, numbers in thousands; and percent change in number of households by type, 1990 to 2000)

percent change 1990–2000

	1980		1990		2000		1990–2000
	number	percent	number	percent	number	percent	percent change
All households	13,980	100.0	21,245	100.0	25,339	100	19.3
Family households	12,221	87.42	17,368	81.8	19,513	77.0	12.4
Marrried couple	9,949	71.17	13,610	64.1	14,947	59.0	9.8
Female householder	1,916	13.71	3,083	14.5	3,632	14.3	17.8
Male householder	356	2.55	675	3.2	934	3.7	38.4
Nonfamily households	1,758	12.58	3,877	18.2	5,826	23.0	50.3
Female householder	598	4.28	1,351	6.4	1,806	7.1	33.7
Male householder	1,160	8.30	2,526	11.9	4,020	15.9	59.1

Source: 1990–1991 Almanac of Consumer Markets published by American Demographics Press

*Charts reprinted from **The Boomer Report***

CHAPTER 8

Boomer Politics

A contradiction in terms

Evidence of diminishing political loyalty and interest is clear for anyone to see. During the last four presidential elections the voter count was down. For years, we've had a Republican president, but a Congress controlled by Democrats. Those who toe the mark of a strict party line seem to have vanished like the wind. Democrats win in stalwart Republican districts; Republicans win in those formerly private domains of their Democrat counterparts. Labels that used to be definitions now serve to disguise and not edify. Nowadays, one can't tell a liberal from a conservative. What one can tell, is that apathy is the boomer mind-set, or rather, the lack of political mind-set.

Many older members of the population who went

dutifully to the polls are not even alive anymore. They, of course, have been replaced by boomers, who, after all, make up one-third of our country's population. What these oldsters have not been replaced by is *voters*. Boomers have not been inspired to get out there and participate in elections.

We've been told in excruciating detail of the scandal in the savings and loan industry, aided and abetted by members of the United States Senate. We read about toilet seats that cost a small fortune and government-funded studies to find out why small children topple from their trikes. In the midst of a recession, Congress voted itself a hefty raise, and we are treated to whining complaints by public servants who tell us we really shouldn't expect good people to be attracted to serve when the compensation is too low. It's a cinch one doesn't have to be a rocket scientist to know junkets are mostly the first four letters, JUNK–that citizens have to pay for regardless of whether the trips and the knowledge or influence gained by them will ultimately benefit long-suffering and overburdened tax payers.

As a possible bright spot on an otherwise dark horizon, consider the growing influence of third parties. While they haven't taken over much of the power of government, they appear to be nibbling slowly but surely away at major party vote tallies. When C-SPAN offered viewers gavel-to-gavel coverage of the Libertarian Party's presidential nominating convention this summer, it perhaps didn't realize it was showing a remarkably young and politically active group comprised of, you guessed it, a too-small, predominantly boomer army wanting to change the world. That party's suggestion that "None of the above" be placed on all ballots may be the one issue to unite all voters and get them to the polls. If we haven't voted the rascals out, this could be one means to avoid voting the rascals in!

Evidence that boomers don't act as a bloc, yet, comes from an article concerning the formation last year of the American Association of Boomers, based in Texas. AAB claimed a membership this year of just about 11,000. The group was founded by certified public accountant, Karen Meredith. She is trying to swell the ranks in hopes boomers will coalesce to deal with some pressing major issues, such as the dwindling Social Security community pot, the burgeoning national debt and failed public education. Lobbying for tax reforms and learning how to manage their finances are two other primary areas for this group. Were it not for boomers' individualism and distrust of mainstream politics, the founder believes AAB would by now be a much larger organization.

In the August '91 *Seattle Times/Seattle Post Intelligencer,* Meredith discussed the things she and boomer AAB members in all fifty states talk about when they meet. According to the writer, Marsha King, "When Meredith meets with boomers from across the country, we rant and rave about the 'despicable' government, the way it lies and spends our money." AAB is among the organizations pushing for limiting congressional terms. As in all such meetings, discussion is free-wheeling, and covers a myriad of boomer concerns. Much time is spent mulling family relationships, shared concerns about echo boomers, and musings on their own health and job situations. Ms. King quoted other authors, ministers, demographers and researchers on boomers. They seem to share a positive, but realistic outlook on boomers and the effect they are going to have. Boomers are seen moving away from the "Me" generation and want to be taken seriously both as a group and as individuals. Those interviewed for the article, *Boomer Angst,* see boomers eventually taking control of politics and instituting a return to important values. The fact that boomers want it now may act as a plus. They've been used to getting their own way, and, if they get their own way in the political arena, that well could benefit boomer and non-boomer alike. If this taking charge takes off, it will be a trend worth watching.

I want to be wary of stepping out on a limb here, but this group's membership has almost doubled from last year's 6,000. Politicians, take heed. If this group swells to even a tiny fraction of the total boomer population, things in local council chambers, in state houses and in Washington, D.C., are going to undergo some changes.

When the group's membership was surveyed on significant political issues, it revealed a strong conservative approach to fiscal matters and an equally strong liberal stance on individual rights. Politicos are keeping a wary eye on this group. If it grows into a voting bloc, there would be more than a few of those career politicians turned out of office to be replaced by boomers with an emerging political agenda and shared political consciousness.

Other issue-oriented minority parties may be smart enough to appeal to the boomers and their concern about things that matter to them, such as the environment, ecology, health care for the elderly and decent schools for their children, for example. I doubt, though, that boomers are going to be as easily influenced as their folks were. As I've said, we're dealing with better educated citizens who will have an impact on how this world is run, even if they don't turn out in droves to vote for change.

Will boomers really be able to have some impact on the environment without voting to force change? The answer is a resounding "Yes." Boomers are leading the pack in that area. They're asking for, make that demanding, products kind to the earth and gentle to their fellow creatures. More than half of them recycle paper, glass and cans, and an equal number avoid buying products with a host of unpronounceable additives. Sales of bottled water have exceeded all expectations as boomers became concerned about just what *was* coming from their taps.

Only a few months before this book went to press, there was an election in San Diego to fill four important city council slots. Those races were decided by an abysmal 23% of the voters who made it to the polls. Low turnout is not a new phenomenon but it is gaining more attention and causing more concern. Do not assume that as boomers get older they will automatically and obediently go to the polls.

One of the things you have to remember is that the boomer, especially the older ones, came out of the revolutionary '60s, times that changed our country dramatically.

Many boomers were old enough to be aware of the assassinations of a president and a civil rights advocate. Boomers weren't old enough to vote when John F. Kennedy was elected in 1960, but they were old enough to watch television to see him shot. Television showed them Watts burning in the long hot summer of 1965. Boomers felt the effects of Lyndon Johnson and the Vietnam War, and when they did reach voting age they showed their disgust at the war, and by their vocal protests, made it obvious LBJ was not going to be voted in for a second full term. They have carried these political memories with them into adulthood.

When the war in Vietnam escalated in 1964, that was the same year that 27 million boomers became eligible for the draft. Approximately one-third were drafted, and about one-tenth actually served in Vietnam. More than 47,000 were killed during the conflict; many of those were boomers. Is it any wonder protests were the order of the day on college campuses? Kids weren't kids anymore—they were cannon fodder and they knew it. The war finally ended in 1975, two years after the cease fire.

They saw the Watergate crisis and watched the man who was "not a crook" resign the highest office in the land in 1974. One might reasonably expect them to be more interested in the political process than past generations. The opposite is, however, painfully true, causing some to be concerned that politics and government may become the province only of special interest groups, or worse, extremists. As boomers are such an individualistic group, the reasons for the lack of interest in political matters are likely to be quite diverse. While some of them were inserting flowers into gun barrels, others volunteered or were drafted and marched off to fight. Many were too young to know what war even meant during the JFK and LBJ years. Those who saw the horror of Vietnam still may view government as the cause of conflict, certainly not the cure. Sure, hosts of boomers and baby busters, those born from 1965 to 1977, participated in the Persian Gulf War as proud members of the military. Don't forget the others. Boomers, busters and echo boomers were also quite visible in their opposition to that quick-fix solution to long-standing problems in the oil-rich Middle East.

As they became more aware of the world around them, boomers were perhaps a bit disappointed (and also ironically amused) as they watched their parents accept tired old political platitudes, and continue to elect the kind of political hacks who made the same old pie-in-the-sky promises they always had in exchange for "X" on the ballot next to their names. It was obvious to the boomer that things weren't changing for the better. They were changing for the worse. Cliches did not equal cure, and the boomers saw the truth of that too graphically on television and in the newspapers as they grew up and formed political opinions.

So, among the things boomers don't share with their

parents are brand loyalty and an inclination to stick with just one political party because of some unquestioning faith in the system. It used to be, if one's parents and grandparents voted as Democrats, Republicans or Independents, their children would be likely to do the same. This is not the case today. If the American Association of Boomers has anything to say about it, members will join forces and ballots to limit the number of terms that may be served by members of Congress. That group is also plenty angry about the loss of the few retirement options and tax benefits available to boomers. When Individual Retirement Accounts went kaput and the marriage deduction was axed, AAB became a reality. Founder Karen Meredith just wants to even the score so members of AAB get the same consideration and wield as much clout as members of AARP!

In April 1990, *The Boomer Report* included the following, that I've taken the liberty to quote in part, "AAB vs. AARP: The Alphabet Battle of the Century? Will boomers clash with seniors?. . . Many of the things they (boomers) want to preserve for generations coming up are exactly the same things AARP wants." The article presents the sobering fact that the first of the boomers will be eligible to join AARP in fewer than five years!

Boris Yeltsin stood on a tank and Mikhail Sergevich Gorbachev survived a coup. How then can there be a lack of interest in political matters? In the August 20, '91 USA TODAY interview, before the coup was over, economist Jim Williams explained that the coup would fail because it was a reaction of the older Soviet generation. Russian boomers are ready to move away from communism, he said. They wouldn't buy into the attitudes of their parents and grandparents. They preferred to learn from their peers. It is his opinion that boomers are "very moral and very selfish" and that they are taking over a "moral revolution" as was experienced in the Soviet Union. Apparently, boomers are an international breed with a universal mind-set.

In spite of a fallen Berlin Wall and a breakaway trio severed from the Union of Soviet Socialist Republics, there is still a frightening apathy. When the Goddess of Liberty was toppled in China, didn't you expect interest in politics to soar? So did I, and that interest did soar, but only for a painfully short period. During the short duration of the Persian Gulf War there did seem to be heightened awareness, but as soon as our desire for instant gratification was satisfied by a speedy victory, apathy reigned once more. Polls of high school and college students reveal an appalling ignorance of politics coupled with an alarming lack of interest. Are boomers doing any better? No. More than 50% of them say they have no interest in politics. That same percentage stays away from the voting booths. If echo boomers continue this trend, there'll be little need for extra voting precincts.

Can marketing offer solutions to the pressing problem of voter apathy? As a marketer, I have to say yes, but it's a qualified yes. The education ball has been dropped with a resounding thud. Classes in political science, history, American institutions and the like are dreaded. They're seen as excruciatingly dull, and in many cases, they are. Subjects filled with the potential to excite and inflame young minds are taught by rote and are seen by students as interminable boredom. For boomers to take action, there has to be a real or perceived benefit to them. A major educational effort will have to be made to show boomers they need to take part in the political process, if only in self defense. Traditionally, older members of the country's electorate do go out to the polls and do get out the vote, and those factors make for a concentration of power in too few hands, always a dangerous situation. In the case of "oldsters" versus "boomers," it could get sticky once boomers start to act as they are, the majority!

They may well need to act to protect themselves. In January '91, *Changing Times* reported the likelihood of additional taxes, even on retirement income, to help fatten the social security coffers. Reiterated in the article is the wry observation that "baby boomers are notoriously skeptical about social security." (So what else is new?) As the push toward later retirement gathers steam, some see age 72 as the target. Boomers will have to work longer to collect anything at all. This will be compounded when they put less into the system than benefits being paid out. The plus mentioned in the piece dealt with the possible lifting of the "earnings test" that takes away a buck for every two earned by Social Security recipients.

Musings that boomers may become more politically involved as their children get older deserve some scrutiny. Not too long ago, groups of more affluent boomers were formed to work for children's rights. In so many families, Mom and Dad were not joined by a little stranger until their careers were on track and they felt financially secure enough to have children. These older parents sought support from their peers in dealing with questions about education, child care, health care. Energized boomers became super parents who, because they are generally well-educated, knew the questions to ask, and were smart enough to dismiss or reject superficial solutions.

The fact that boomers are interested in their children does not mean they will turn to the political process for solutions to problems concerning them. Boomers don't have that much faith in the political system to start with. If the voter count is down because boomers don't participate, what do you think boomers' children are going to do when they reach voting age? From where I'm viewing the situation, echo boomers will also pick up on their parents' political mind-set and reject the political process.

I don't agree that consumption necessarily means boomers are greedy and think only of themselves, but it is a good sign to see them taking such an active role in respect to their children. In fact, countless boomers do amazing volunteer work with children—in schools' literacy programs and as hospital volunteers, to name just two. Boomer parents are coming more and more to believe they have a responsibility to "give back" to their communities, and an even more pressing responsibility to teach their children some good old-fashioned values.

In light of the above, how are politicians going to get the boomer vote? More correctly, how are they going to get boomers involved? If office seekers pay attention to my marketing techniques that work for any product or service, they have a good chance. What it's going to take is easy in theory, difficult in practice. Politicians have to state their messages simply. They have to understand boomers are not going to be hauled into the voting net like a school of mindless fish. Boomers will have to be marketed for political action not by their ages, but by their individual and very diverse interests and concerns.

Selling politics isn't really that much different from selling hotel rooms. Where politicians are promising to do service for the general public, the hotel industry does the same thing. The major difference is that at least with hotels, you have some idea of what you will be getting when you get there, and with politicians you know only what is promised. You don't have to return to a hotel that doesn't live up to your expectations. Once someone is elected, however, you are stuck with him or her and have to wait too long to remedy the situation by recalling or voting the person out!

For politicians to be successful, they have to remember everything said in the previous chapters. The boomer is an individualistic person and politicians cannot keep basing their campaigns on the negative aspects of their opponents. Hitting on negatives is not a good sell to the boomer. Without using scare tactics that boomers see right through, candidates need to "sell" the strengths of their own platforms by stressing what they can do for this country to make a better United States and a better world for all of us to inhabit. It's a tall order. No matter how good the intentions of politicians are, boomers don't truly believe they are capable of carrying out their programs and cleaning up the stable of political messes. To convince them to the contrary is going to take enthusiastic dedication.

Boomers aren't going to care if a candidate has smoked a little pot, dropped a tab of acid, or protested any war. What they are looking for is candidates who recognize the potential power of the boomer, and who don't insult their intelligence by making promises impossible to keep. Boomers are not stupid. Candidates will have to work very hard to convince boomers that their promises are somehow different from all the rest. They will have to struggle to overcome past and recent history of shattered campaign promises. They will have to prove they won't be compromised by deals and pressure from their colleagues.

Political messages need to be repeated over and over again to get and keep boomers' attention. It wouldn't hurt any candidate to take a communications lesson from a recent president. When talking to citizens became the norm and replaced lectern-pounding speeches, people listened. I think they want to listen again. Boomers won't care what politicians have said and done to entice their parents. Politicians have to entice the boomers, and if this isn't done soon, they will never become active participants in the political process, they will do it by themselves and for themselves.

It won't hurt their causes if candidates are boomers themselves! And as boomers are a huge segment of our population—a majority of our voting population—it stands to reason more and more of them will enter the political arena, if only because of a correctly-perceived need to protect themselves. But candidates will have to be wary of imitating boomers in any phony way, and they will have to move cautiously to avoid patronizing this well-educated group of potential supporters. Politicians who can inspire without patronizing can be effective, but they have to speak honestly to boomer concerns. To get this group as fired up as young people were in the '60s is going to take a major switch in candidates' mind-set. Otherwise, boomers will see right through to the cynicism that has hallmarked recent crops of candidates, and those running for office will not be able to reach the radical who was so instrumental in the peace and environmental movements of the past.

Politicians are going to have to change their strategy to accommodate this generation, or they will never capture the boomer vote. Boomers will have to be told and shown, again and again, what's in it for them and their families. Boomer women, especially, will have to be convinced that the election of a particular office-seeker will be of benefit to them and their children. After all, 51% of the boomers born are women, and they will have to be considered carefully, and on an intellectual as well as emotional level. Blind faith voting is a thing of the past, and I, for one, won't miss that. Marketers have to reach out to boomers more often to convince and keep them convinced, and that holds true if you're selling them a product, a service, or giving them a chance to vote you into (or your opponent out of) office!

The January-February issue of *My Generation,* the American Association of Boomers newsletter, included some sage advice in a lengthy quote from Generations by William Strauss and Neil Howe. The book includes a message to each of the four unique generations that are still living in the United States, and also have identified a "Four generation cycle (Idealistic, Reactive, Civic and Adaptive) which has continued to repeat itself century after century."

It appears that boomers may finally have been recognized for their idealism and potential. The authors write of this remarkable group that it ". . . will someday leave a decisive mark on civilization quite unlike anything they have done up to now." I think their idealism will triumph and I hope I'm around to see boomers truly come into their own.

Now for a little fun. Although the intent of this book is serious, and I sincerely hope will be helpful to boomers and those who market and advertise products and services to them, I think the following will let you lighten up a bit before you go out to conquer the market with the new knowledge you've gained from this book. The following "Acronym Alert" is from *The Boomer Report,* July, '91.

"As a public service, we bring you an update of the acronym hit parade—that device marketers use to try to pigeonhole the population, mainly the amorphous / elusive boomer."

Buppies	Black Urban Professionals
Dinks	Dual Income, No Kids
Grampies	Growing Retired Active Monied Persons in an Excellent State
Guppies	Gay Urban Professionals
Huppies	Hispanic Urban Professionals
Juppies	Japanese Urban Professionals

Muppies	Mature Urban Professionals
Oinks	One Income, No Kids
Opals	Older People with Active Lifestyles
Puppies	Pregnant Urban Professionals
Smuppies	Saving More Until Post Parenting Years
Yiffies	Young, Individualistic, Freedom-Minded and Few
Yoinks	Young One-Income Couples, No Kids
Yuppies	Young Urban Professionals
Yuppie Puppies	Children of Yuppies
Moss	Middle-aged, Over-stressed, Semi-Affluent Suburbanites

In conclusion, it has been my intention to share my years of boomer marketing experience, knowledge and proven strategic principles with you. However, this useful information will have no value whatsoever unless you condition your own mind as to the consciousness of the boomer mind!

As soon as *you* the marketer accept the fact that boomers as consumers are really and truly different from every other generation in history, and certainly from the current sociological evaluation given them, *you* will reap endless benefit from the ideology I have set forth for you. Just remember the ageless challenge - Sell them if you can!

ACKNOWLEDGMENTS

Above all else, I thank God and praise His glory for making this book possible. Others I want to thank are my brothers, Larry Goodman, who suggested the book's title, and Kent Goodman, the master of all creative advertising, who taught me a lot. I thank my sister Charlotte who always believed in me. I thank my boomer children, Sheri and Michael, who typify this generation. I thank my grandchildren, Jacob and Michelle, who are the echo boomers. Mary Lou - my friend who was great for my research, along with her boomer daughter Desirée.

I thank Andy Fessel, Senior Vice President of Research and Marketing for FOX Network; Paul Lenburg, Executive Vice-President of ASI Market Research Inc.; Ed Schwitzky, Director of Marketing for The Westin La Paloma in Tucson; Bob Moore, Vice-President and General Manager of KQLZ radio in Los Angeles, and Bill Crabtree, Vice- President of Western Region Sales of Gannett Outdoor Network, USA. Of all the magazines, newspaper articles and newsletters used during the writing of this book, I am especially grateful and indebted to Thia Golson and the staff of *The Boomer Report,* for whom I write.

I thank the radio, television and hotel industries for letting me work with them to streetmarket the boomer generation, and my clients, among which are Handlery Hotels in California, the Long Beach Area Convention and Visitors' Council, Outrigger Hotels in Hawaii and on the mainland, The Ramada Renaissance in Long Beach and Los Angeles, The Sheraton Park Central in Dallas and The Westin La Paloma in Tucson; and to Joe Kordsmeier and The Edward Thomas

Company. We've all learned from each other.

Special thanks go to all of the media and hotel associations, organizations and publications that have given me the opportunity to speak to and write for them. Carol, Diana and Triva, my staff at Western Media Corporation, have helped me to achieve the results and success for our clients that initiated my interest to begin researching and working with the boomer generation. Their immeasurable contribution is appreciated, and I thank them sincerely.

And of course, I thank my writer Irene Schaffer and editor Lil Wagner who interpreted my words and helped me put this book together.

And finally, I extend my gratitude to the boomers themselves, whose mind-set has completely fooled just about everyone who has written and spoken about this unique generation. Boomers and their children will change the course of marketing history and you will discover that Rock 'n' Roll will live forever...!